Coaching and Mentoring in Education

Palgrave Teaching and Learning

Series Editor: **Sally Brown**

Coaching and Mentoring in Higher Education
Facilitating Work-Based Learning
Facilitating Workshops
For the Love of Learning
Fostering Self-Efficacy in Higher Education Students
Leading Dynamic Seminars
Learning, Teaching and Assessment in Higher Education
Learning with the Labyrinth
Live Online Learning
Masters Level Teaching, Learning and Assessment

Further titles are in preparation

Universities into the 21st Century

Series Editors: **Noel Entwistle and Roger King**

Becoming an Academic
Cultures and Change in Higher Education
Global Inequalities and Higher Education
Learning Development in Higher Education
Managing your Academic Career
Managing your Career in Higher Education Administration
Research and Teaching
Teaching Academic Writing in UK Higher Education
Teaching for Understanding at University
Understanding the International Student Experience
The University in the Global Age
Writing in the Disciplines

Palgrave Research Skills

Authoring a PhD
The Foundations of Research (2nd edn)
Getting to Grips with Doctoral Research
Getting Published
The Good Supervisor (2nd edn)
Maximizing the Impacts of University Research
The PhD Viva
Planning Your Postgraduate Research PhD by Published Work
The Postgraduate Research Handbook (2nd edn)
The Professional Doctorate
Structuring Your Research Thesis

You may also be interested in:

Teaching Study Skills and Supporting Learning

For a complete listing of all our titles in this area please **visit www.palgrave.com/ studyskills**

Coaching and Mentoring in Higher Education

A Step-by-Step Guide to Exemplary Practice

Jill Andreanoff

First published 2016 by
PALGRAVE

Palgrave in the UK is an imprint of Macmillan Publishers Limited, registered in England, company number 785998, of 4 Crinan Street, London, N1 9XW.

Palgrave is a global imprint of the above companies and is represented throughout the world.

Palgrave® and Macmillan® are registered trademarks in the United States, the United Kingdom, Europe and other countries.

ISBN 978–1–137–45149–1 paperback

This book is printed on paper suitable for recycling and made from fully managed and sustained forest sources. Logging, pulping and manufacturing processes are expected to conform to the environmental regulations of the country of origin.

A catalogue record for this book is available from the British Library.

The author would like to thank Gillian Knibbs who provided not only a case study but a great deal of support, acting as a trusted advisor during the creation of the book.

Many thanks also to the other case study contributors:

Jo Hocking – University of Western Australia
Amy Griggs – University of California
Dr Julie Preston/Jane Emery – University of Tasmania
Adam Rowland – RMIT University

Library of Congress Cataloging-in-Publication Data

Names: Andreanoff, Jill, author.
Title: Coaching and mentoring in higher education : a step-by-step guide to exemplary practice / Jill Andreanoff.
Description: New York : Palgrave Macmillan, 2016. | Series: Palgrave teaching and learning | Includes index.
Identifiers: LCCN 2016002455 | ISBN 9781137451491 (paperback)
Subjects: LCSH: Mentoring in education. | Education, Higher. | BISAC: EDUCATION / Higher. | EDUCATION / Teaching Methods & Materials / General. | STUDY AIDS / Study Guides.
Classification: LCC LB1731.4 .A53 2016 | DDC 371.102—dc23
LC record available at http://lccn.loc.gov/2016002455

Printed and bound by CPI Group (UK) Ltd, Croydon, CR0 4YY

Contents

List of figures and tables

Series editor's preface

Palgrave Teaching and Learning

Coaching and Mentoring in Higher Education

I welcome the publication of this invaluable volume in the Palgrave Teaching and Learning series, designed for all who care about teaching and learning in higher education. The series has the express aim of providing useful, relevant, current and helpful guidance on key issues in learning and teaching in the tertiary/post compulsory education sector at a time when the pace of change is fast and expectations of those involved in teaching and supporting students are increasing. Texts in this series address a range of essential teaching and learning imperatives, with a deliberately international focus, and a determination to offer practical advice and ideas, grounded in scholarship.

At a time when mentoring and coaching are becoming more widely recognised as central to student experience in higher education, this book offers useful guidance both to those new to teaching and support work who are just embarking on this area of work and to those who are already experienced in offering student support in this way, including as it does case studies and examples of good practice from the UK and internationally. The volume is comprehensive, clear and well written, expertly combining theory and practice, and is a very welcome addition to the series.

Sally Brown
August 2015

Introduction

There are continued pressures on higher education institutions to improve their provision and remain or become major competitors within the field. This is driven by financial constraints and increasing student fees which demand a higher level of accountability in student satisfaction. The impact on student expectations and retention, as identified by Foskett, Roberts, & Maringe (2006), has increased the need for higher education institutions to be more creative and diverse in providing support for students and enabling them to succeed.

It has been suggested by many for several years that offering the opportunity to form a supportive relationship with a more experienced student will ease the transition into university and reduce attrition (Pitkethly & Prosser, 2001; Hill & Reddy, 2007). Other studies such as Andrews & Clark (2011) also refer to 'student success' through mentoring in particular. It has also been well reported that mentoring in higher education can help students to cope with the demands of academia, Quinn, Muldoon, & Hollingworth (2002), and have a positive effect for the mentees and mentors, Leidenfrost et al. (2011).

There is plentiful literature on the success of peer support programmes and in particular peer mentoring. It is worth noting that Husband & Jacobs (2009), Andrews & Clark (2011), and Thomas (2012) also identify the need for a well-structured mentoring programme to be in place within higher education institutions in order to obtain optimum results. Peer coaching, although currently not as widely used, is likely to gain momentum as higher education institutions seek alternative methods of enhancing the student experience and improving their academic attainment.

Mentoring and coaching are well-established mechanisms for accelerating learning and attainment in a number of settings from the education to the public and business sectors and are now widely used terms. However, a number of issues have arisen from their becoming more commonly used expressions. A certain amount of confusion appears to have arisen in the definitions of the processes, which has in turn led to broadly publicised misuse of the phrases, 'mentoring' and 'coaching'. The term 'mentoring' for example is often loosely used in popular TV reality shows where contestants are frequently assigned a mentor who tells them what to do, when to do it, and how to do it. Little or no consideration often appears to be given to the views, values, or opinions of the contestants being mentored.

This one-directional type of intervention bears little resemblance to the true supportive nature of a mentoring or coaching relationship, the aim of which is to encourage reflective thinking and decision making in the mentee, leading them to achieve their aims and objectives in a way that is suitable for them. It is this type of two-way relationship that proves to be so valuable to both the learner and the person offering the support. Thorough training for coaches and mentors is crucial to achieving this type of relationship, and when being offered to higher education students, in particular, it enables them to develop effective team leading and communication skills, improving their employability opportunities.

This book will endeavour to define 'best practice' mentoring and coaching and encourage the reader to trust in the well-documented successes of this type of relationship. Adopting these methods rather than the more directional approach is far more likely to lead to self-efficacy and personal development of the mentee or coachee. It is also less likely to result in complaints from participants who have been given 'bad advice' from their mentor or coach, who should in fact refrain, as far as possible, from giving any advice at all.

Mentoring and coaching are becoming more accepted within the higher education sector as a relatively cost effective form of promoting student success. However it may not be as cost effective as one might envisage if practised properly in terms of coordinator time. This can be seen from the Table of Coordinator costs later in Table 2.1 and additional costs to be accounted for in Chapter 4. It is a worthwhile investment, however, when you take into account not only the benefits for those being supported but also those who develop their skills by being trained as a mentor or coach. The pitfalls that I have both encountered and overcome during 15 years' experience of developing and delivering mentoring and coaching programmes within the higher education and other sectors will be shared. This will allow others to avoid making similar mistakes when implementing their own programme.

How to develop both small-scale programmes and much larger ones will be covered along with advice on the possible pitfalls and how to avoid them for both types and sizes of scheme. Case studies and examples of exemplary practice programmes will be provided, from which ideas for your own programme can be drawn. A variety of topics for support will be highlighted, from supporting students with mental health and physical disabilities to alumni mentoring to supporting final-year students in the transition from education to work. The aims and objectives of each of the programmes differ from academic peer coaching for students studying specific subjects (e.g. Accounting and Finance, Law, and Physics) to Technology Mentoring whereby members of staff are supported by students with the objective of improving their learning and use of assistive teaching technologies. Other programmes, such as those specifically designed to support international students in their first year, will also be used as case study examples.

The inclusion of case studies and examples of programme materials and resources will take the readers step by step through the process of setting up their own individual programme. The entire process, from recruitment of mentors and coaches, to inducting the mentees/coachees, to offering supervision, right through to planning and conducting the programme evaluation, will be explored. The reader will be given guidance on the nuances between individual scheme objectives and how to adapt the implementation process to suit. It will be explained, for example, how mentor or coach promotional material can be adapted for different schemes in order to attract students with the desired characteristics and attributes for your intended programme. The methods used for promoting the support to your intended audience is also imperative to prevent it from appearing patronising or unattractive and to ensure that the participants are fully engaged from the onset. It is seemingly small details such as these that can have a huge impact on whether a scheme succeeds or not.

The first part of the book explores the various ways in which coaching and mentoring can be utilised and exactly what is meant by the terms in the context of this book. Appendix 1 provides a questionnaire that can be used in conjunction with this book to help plan your exemplary practice programme. The second part is devoted to the planning and implementation of your programme. This includes everything from identifying the need, securing funding, the possible costs, the training programme, and the recruitment process for mentors, coaches, and the intended learners through to the final evaluation process.

The final chapters are devoted to more specialised programmes such as ementoring, school-pupil-based mentoring, using university students as mentors, to possible accreditation for the mentors or coaches.

1 What Are Mentoring and Coaching?

There is much conflict about the terms 'mentoring' and 'coaching' and the difference between them. Whilst the actual definitions of mentoring or coaching are not absolutely crucial to the implementation of a programme, serious consideration should be given to this prior to scheme implementation as it will become important when it comes to the training and preparation of your intended participants. Jacobi (1991) first recognised the need for a precise definition of peer support terms in order to determine the necessary elements for success. The debate on the differences between these two interventions still continues and is likely to do so for some time, with authors such as Chao (2006) critiquing others for not sufficiently defining the terms.

Coaching and mentoring are more usually one-to-one relationships and although the mentors and coaches should be supported throughout the process, this should be carried out through regular supervision rather than observation. A scheme coordinator should not normally impose any pre-planned structure or format to the sessions. Group mentoring is sometimes implemented, although this arguably could be labelled 'peer-assisted learning' or 'supplemental instruction', both of which are discussed later. Bearing in mind that mentoring and coaching are usually and best 'client led', group mentoring can be difficult when the clients' needs are all different. A case study example is provided in Chapter 12 of a 'Raising Aspirations' pupil mentoring programme that consists of a mixture of group and one-to-one sessions, demonstrating how the different approaches can be combined. Pupils are mentored in small groups for up to 12 weeks and, in addition, have alternate one-to-one sessions with the mentor, enabling more personal issues to be discussed in private. The group sessions are comprised of loosely pre-planned topics that are designed to promote discussion about the merits of obtaining a good education and expectations of studying at university. Group mentoring is more commonly used for school pupils and young people.

As was mentioned in the introduction, it is strongly advised that a unidirectional type of relationship should be avoided at all costs. Unfortunately, mentoring, to a number of people merely consists of a more experienced person advising a younger, less experienced one on the basis of his or her own experiences. Not only does this approach bring with it the danger of the mentor giving poor advice, resulting in possible complaints when the advice given does not meet the expectations or needs of the mentee, but it also encourages dependence. In addition it is likely to impede self-development, decision making, and reflective thinking in the mentee or coachee. What is also often overlooked with this form of intervention is the fact that just because someone is older and has more experience, it does not always follow that their advice in the given situation is best for the learner. Particularly if there is a large age gap, things might have changed since the mentor was 'in their shoes'; moreover this approach does not take into account the individuality of human beings in general. What may be sound advice for one person is not necessarily the right path for someone else to follow. Adopting this approach often encourages applications from volunteer mentors who wish to relive their careers and education through their mentees.

Self-efficacy has been shown to be an indicator of success, particularly within the context of higher education and beyond where autonomy and independence of students are vital (Crozier 1997; Sander et al. 2009). In view of this, a less directional and more facilitative approach will allow the mentee to develop these skills and thought processes to a greater degree. By teaching your selected mentors and coaches to ask good open and exploratory questions, explore various available options, action plan, and give feedback, the need to give advice is kept to an absolute minimum. The content of the training sessions is crucial to success, and the individual elements will be fully covered in Chapter 6. This facilitative rather than directive approach will also be more likely to engage the learners when used with methods and approaches that best suit them and their particular circumstances.

Mentors and coaches should always be aware that everyone is an individual; that people approach their 'problems' in different ways; and that no specific method or path is correct. The role of a mentor or coach should be to discover the right method for a particular person, allowing individuals to reach their chosen goals at their own pace and in a way that suits them. It is this skilled process that leads to achievement, success and improved performance. In addition, the processes that have been learned through their mentor or coach can be utilised long after the mentoring or coaching programme has finished. Using this method may also lead to further development of the mentor or coach, as they too may discover new approaches to problem solving from their learner.

There is far less literature on peer coaching within a higher education context, but again the definitions differ from author to author. Some, such as Huston & Weaver (2008), describe the process as a collegial and voluntary one to improve or expand their approaches to teaching, and others, such as

Cox (2012), use a broader definition where the coaching is not restricted to the development of improved classroom techniques and the participants take turns to coach each other. Two different models of coaching are described by Ackland (1991) as the 'expert' model and the 'reciprocal' model. Each is described as a different process with differing aims and objectives that range from transferring training to practice to resolving a problematic state. Donegan et al. (2000) describe the coaching process as an expert teacher giving support and feedback and making suggestions to untrained or less skilled peers, which would indicate a more directive approach.

Parsloe et al. (2000) discuss the various definitions of coaching and mentoring and state that the general consensus appears to be that mentoring is instructional whilst coaching is nondirective. They do admit, however, that the boundaries are not firmly set. Ives (2008) discusses the different approaches used in coaching in differing contexts and concludes that some approaches strongly discourage advice giving whilst others suggest that coaching requires guidance. Stober et al. (2006) agree that the term coaching, alongside mentoring, has become increasingly difficult to define.

What is apparent in these discussions regarding the definitions of coaching and mentoring is that there still remains a lack of clarity. However, for the context of this book it is advised, for the previously cited reasons, that a nondirective approach should be used for both coaching and mentoring programmes.

What can help differentiate mentoring from coaching is the length of the intervention and the aims and objectives of your intended programme. Mentoring is quite often defined as a longer-term intervention given over a period of a year or so whilst coaching is very often offered for a shorter duration. Mentoring is also often perceived as a more holistic approach than coaching, the latter being more usually focussed on a specific goal such as academic improvement or work performance.

Another factor that needs some consideration is the people who are being targeted for support – from here onwards referred to as the 'learners'. Again, depending on the context, some view mentoring as a deficit model, required when someone is failing to do as well as they could or underperforming, whilst coaching can be understood to be for those who are talented and need some investment to progress even faster. Interestingly the opposite is true within other organisations and cultures, and so some preliminary enquiries as to how mentoring and coaching are perceived within your own organisation could be crucial to the success and uptake of your programme. If, for example, mentoring is viewed within your organisation as a deficit model, possibly as a result of previous attempts to introduce a similar type of support, then it may be prudent to introduce the support as coaching.

There is also a vast difference in cultures between and within different nations, and so it is essential that when setting up your own programme, some knowledge of the context and existing culture is explored and taken into account. It will also be valuable to conduct some research with your intended beneficiaries to elicit their views on whether coaching or mentoring might be useful to them.

Within my own institution, a similar peer support programme was much more widely sought after when offered as 'peer coaching' than when it had been promoted as 'mentoring' the previous year. This may have been the result of previous mentoring schemes offered within the institution to widening participation students (those from lower socioeconomic backgrounds) and those with disabilities or mental health issues. However, other factors may have been the promotional materials and wording used to advertise the peer support offered. This situation illustrates the importance of knowing the historical background of both the organisation and the wider community when implementing a coaching or mentoring programme. The case study for this programme can be found on page 119.

The final requirement for a successful programme and a thriving mentoring or coaching relationship is to ensure that the mentors or coaches do not have any vested interest in their allocated learner that could cause a conflict of interest. Whilst it might initially appear that it would be useful for the coach or mentor to have some background information about their allocated learner, it could, in fact, impede rapport building. Too many assumptions or pre-judgements could easily be made by the mentor or coach. When the learner is in some way appraised or assessed by the coach or mentor, it may also act as a deterrent to openness and honesty. Clutterbuck et al. (1999) describe this as 'offline' help, and it is this capacity of the mentor or coach to remain completely detached about any given situation presented to them that is key to success. For example it would be far more difficult for learners to talk openly about feelings of being overwhelmed with their workload or not getting on with their peers when talking to a coach who will later be appraising them either in a working or other capacity.

Whilst all the above factors do need to be considered, it is strongly suggested that any definition for your programme should adhere to the following guidelines:

- ▶ A nondirective approach should be adopted whether the scheme is labelled coaching or mentoring.
- ▶ No pre-planned schedule for the sessions should be provided for the coaches and mentors (except perhaps where the scheme is targeted at young people under 16 years).

▶ The sessions should consist of one-to-one meetings (with the possible exception of the scheme targeted at younger people or pupils).

▶ The relationship offered should be 'offline', and the learner should not be a direct 'reportee' of their allocated coach or mentor.

▶ The relationship should be deemed confidential between the coach or mentor and the learner without input or reporting back on the content of meetings to other stakeholders (except in the event of disclosure issues).

It is also essential to ensure that under no circumstances should the support be offered as a 'counselling' or as a 'therapeutic' intervention, as the majority of higher education institutions will have such a dedicated service in place. The mentor's or coach's role in such cases would be to signpost their learners to a therapy or counselling service should they have needs that require help of a more therapeutic nature. How to cope with this type of situation should be included as part of the mentor or coach training.

▶ Other Forms of Peer Support

There does appear to be more consensus about other forms of peer support such as 'peer-assisted learning', which is described more usually as using trained second-year or third-year students ('PAL Leaders'), working alone or in pairs, to regularly supervise the learning of a small group of younger or less able students (Boud 1999; Green 2011; Capstick 2003). Peer-assisted learning is reported to offer an environment in which the younger, less experienced students can benefit in a number of ways. Peer-assisted learning is also more often a structured process and, if well practised, supported by academics or programme tutors. Whilst there is evidence to suggest that this form of peer support is undoubtedly beneficial, it is not the type of programme that is discussed within the confines of this book.

Peer tutoring is another type of support, described by Topping (1996) as an old practice whereby able students work in pairs or in groups with less able students. Peer tutoring is also seen to have high curriculum content and utilises structured materials. Topping goes on to describe nine different types of peer tutoring to suit different circumstances, from cross-year tutoring to reciprocal peer tutoring. Colvin et al. (2010) describe peer tutoring as similar to 'supplemental instruction', whereby more advanced students help less experienced students with course content. Clearly these interventions can be fairly easily distinguished as different from a one-to-one mentoring or coaching relationship, as there will be a clear structure to the sessions from the outset.

Whilst this text is aimed specifically at those implementing a coaching or mentoring programme, many of the suggested procedures for exemplary practice would be the same even if setting up a group support intervention. The training for peer supporters would have a different emphasis and would include instruction on managing small groups as well as planning and preparing for the group support sessions. However, the advice on recruitment, promotion, and evaluation would be similar to that for a mentoring and coaching programme and so may also be of value to those planning group sessions.

▶ The Skills Required for Coaching and Mentoring

The skill set required for mentors and coaches will differ depending on the aims and objectives for your particular programme. For example, if the aim and objective of a peer mentoring programme is to improve the academic attainment of students who are not performing well academically, then it would make no sense to recruit students who are themselves not performing well in this area. They may well have personal skills that would stand them in good stead for a mentoring role, such as good listening and communication skills, but if they have not achieved sufficiently high grades then they will probably not be terribly beneficial in helping you to achieve your aims and objectives.

There are however some key competencies that are essential to either a mentoring or coaching role, and these should be tested at the recruitment stage and throughout the interview and training process.

Good listening skills are key to a mentoring and coaching role. Many people view themselves as good listeners when in fact they actually prefer speaking, and this can often be detected at the interview stage. Your interview questions should be aimed at uncovering specific examples of how they have proven to be 'good listeners' as opposed to them just stating that they are good listeners. If you have candidates with good listening skills, then it will be relatively easy to turn them into active listeners with thorough training.

For most schemes an altruistic nature is usually a welcome quality, and again examples of this can be looked for at the application and interview stages. For many programmes monetary rewards for your mentors and coaches will not be viable within the budgetary constraints, and so many people will be volunteering for the reward of the self-satisfaction of helping others alone. However, the other rewards that being a mentor or coach can bring should not be overlooked and should be well promoted when advertising the role. These will include enhanced communication skills (as part of the training) and, for students particularly, an opportunity to enhance their CVs and gain a personal reference upon successful completion of the programme. As mentoring and coaching are so well utilised in so many sectors from voluntary to private and corporate, being able to include this experience on job and work placement applications can be a real bonus as it is an indicator of leadership qualities too.

There does need to be a good balance between the gains that the applicants want for themselves and what they are prepared to put into it. It would be advisable, for example, to be wary of selecting any applicant who asks at interview exactly when and how much he or she will be paid or when he or she can use you as a referee without showing any genuine interest in the role itself.

Another factor to take into account is available time which is something that the reader will need to consider when deciding from where they will try to recruit their coaches or mentors. It may be that a particular group of people would be best placed to offer the support in terms of knowledge and experience. However, if they are unlikely to be able to spare sufficient time to commit to the programme, then it might be better to select the participants from another group who may have less knowledge and experience but are likely to be more incentivised by the opportunity and have more time to fully commit. What is essential is to raise awareness of the time commitment from the outset, not only for the training days but for the one-to-one sessions as well as attendance at regular support workshops. In a student mentoring programme, for example, a good guideline would be that the students are coping reasonably well with their studies (so don't have modules to retake) and that they are not employed on a paid basis for more than 20 hours per week. If they are working more than this and studying for a full-time degree, they will likely be over-stretching themselves no matter how eager or suitable they are to take part. You would likely be doing them a disservice if you were to select them, and if you did they may become overburdened once matched and withdraw, which would prove damaging to your programme overall.

Due to the many misconceptions surrounding coaching and mentoring, readers can also expect some applicants to apply so that they 'can offer someone, less experienced, the benefit of their advice, wisdom, and opinion'. If handled correctly these applicants can either be deterred in the first instance or, better still, they can be properly trained to offer support using a more facilitative approach, as previously discussed.

A final consideration is the balance of female to male mentors who apply, and some consideration needs to be given to the consequences of a possible imbalance. It may be that an imbalance is perfectly acceptable for your scheme, particularly if it is targeted at a specific gender such as engaging more female students to apply for male-dominated courses. However, if your target audience is likely to be mixed, then you should try to ensure a good balance of male and female mentors or coaches. Sometimes female applicants are more numerous, but steps can be taken when promoting the programme to ensure that male applicants are also attracted to apply. In general male applicants are usually keener to obtain the more practical benefits of taking part, such as obtaining a reference and CV enhancement, though this is not always the case. How to promote your programme to attract the desired applicants will be discussed further in Chapter 5.

Other qualities that should be sought when recruiting your mentors and coaches are good overall communication skills. A certain degree of articulateness is essential for coaches and mentors as they may be communicating and interpreting sometimes complex situations. It will be useful if they are able to express themselves fully, even if they do not possess an extensive vocabulary. In some cases, in particular in a pupil mentoring scheme, a mentor may not so easily be able to establish rapport with their allocated pupils if they speak too eloquently. The best mentors and coaches are those who can easily adapt their communication style to that of their allocated learner.

Self-confidence is another factor that is important for a potential mentor or coach. However, too much confidence can be off-putting for some learners who may feel threatened by an overly confident coach or mentor. A certain degree of skill is required in the matching process to ensure that very confident and extrovert coaches and mentors are not matched with extremely introverted learners, although in some cases (depending on scheme requirements) this may actually be required. Moreover, allowances should always be made for those who are less confident at the application stage. It has become apparent over many years in the recruitment of many mentors and coaches that sometimes an applicant who appears to be very lacking in confidence can actually develop into a powerful mentor or coach. It is a frequently reported fact that the coaches and mentors themselves gain confidence in their own abilities through the experience of supporting others. The process of mentoring or coaching allows them to reveal a breadth of knowledge that they have acquired but of which they may previously have been unaware. Conversely, in some cases, the more confident applicants realise that they are not as knowledgeable as they initially thought. Fortunately, for both kinds of coach or mentor, this type of self-development can be an extremely beneficial learning experience. Extremes in levels of confidence should, nonetheless, be avoided. It is worth noting that overly confident applicants do also tend to be the type to steer towards giving advice and generally have a preference for speaking rather than listening.

▶ **Other Mentor or Coach Attributes**

In a mentoring programme to support students with a disability, for example, would it be essential or helpful if the mentors themselves had a disability? Is it feasible to match your disabled learners with a mentor who has the same disability? Supposing you did decide to match disabilities, will it be possible to recruit mentors with the 'right' disability and foresee what disabilities the students who apply would have? Of course it will be virtually impossible to predict who is going to apply and ethically inappropriate to attempt to recruit the 'right' type of mentor. It might be somewhat patronising to assume that a student with a specific disability would want to be supported by someone with a similar disability, but in practice this may be exactly what happens. One student who was a wheelchair user did actively seek a mentor who was also a wheelchair user. The match was found in this particular case but might quite well not have been practicable. The case study of a disability mentoring programme on page 25 covers many obstacles such as these.

With an academic support scheme it is likely that the learners will want to be matched specifically with a coach or mentor studying the same or similar courses or even perhaps those undertaking similar optional modules. It would also be essential for the mentors or coaches employed on a scheme such as this to be achieving well academically. The criteria could be set as only accepting those who are achieving on average a 2:1 or above. In one scheme where the mentors were expected to support school pupils (who were specifically underachieving in English and Maths), the criterion was set for the mentors to have achieved a good grade in at least one of these subjects whilst at school.

It may be that experience of a particular context or field is useful for your intended programme. For an alumni programme where the mentors were expected to help guide final-year undergraduates into employment, the criterion could be set as having been employed, postgraduation, for a minimum of two years.

For more specific agendas such as encouraging females into male-dominated courses, it is likely that females studying those courses will be your desired mentors. Once this criterion has been set, then you can commence the recruitment process.

2 The Role of the Scheme Coordinator

The role of the mentoring or coaching scheme coordinator is usually vastly underestimated, and a common problem is a lack of allocated hours to implement the programme. Too often, the coordinator is required to set up a new programme in addition to a full-time 'day job'. Not investing sufficient coordinator hours to the programme will however inevitably lead to shortcuts being taken and to a programme that falls short of best practice. This in turn will impact on the success factor and so, if a decision is made to implement a mentoring or coaching programme, then it is essential that the commitment includes appropriate staffing levels and a sufficient allocation of hours. Table 2.1 gives some guidelines on the number of hours required for a typical mentoring or coaching programme.

Table 2.1 Guidelines on Hours Required to Deliver a Coaching or Mentoring Programme

Type of Programme	Number of Mentors/ Coaches	Number of Mentees/ Coachees	Coordinator Hours
School Pupil Mentoring	30	150 (in 5 schools)	600 over 20 weeks
Staff Mentoring	18	24	250 over 30 weeks
Alumni E-Mentoring	50	50	360 over 40 weeks
Peer Coaching for Undergraduates	90	160	500 over 35 weeks

By estimating the number of hours needed to deliver your specific scheme it will then be possible to account for this in your projections. A simple multiplication of your specific hourly coordinator rate times the number of hours to be worked will result in the figure that should be allowed within your budget. Obviously there will be other costs associated with the delivery of your project that will need to be taken into account such as any payments to coaches or mentors and resources, but this will be covered in Chapter 4.

The role of the coordinator is demanding and more often than not, 'front loaded'. The assumption is often made that once the mentors or coaches are recruited, trained, and matched, then the role of the coordinator becomes somewhat redundant. This is a common misconception which can lead to the danger of the relationships dwindling away or not progressing as they should. The role of the coordinator, post-matching, is vital and will consist of the provision of appropriate supervision for the mentors or coaches (based upon monitoring feedback from the participants) and the collection and compilation of mid-way and final evaluation feedback. Regular monitoring of the developing relationships is essential to avert any emerging issues from escalating into more serious ones. Monitoring the frequency of the mentoring or coaching meetings is necessary to ensure that any that are declining are adequately supervised and that mentors or coaches are responding to each others' messages as they should. In the event of ementoring, particularly where an ementoring platform is utilised, regular monitoring of the quality of the emails should also be part of the coordinator's role. Ementoring programmes are covered more fully in Chapter 11.

Even the most exuberant of participants may become embroiled in their work or studies after being matched and forget to respond to a request for a meeting. With busy lives time slips by very quickly, and without a tactful reminder from a coordinator so much time can slip by that it becomes increasingly awkward to make contact. Knowing that a coordinator will be regularly checking up on them is usually sufficient incentive for mentors, coaches, and learners to maintain the agreed contact schedule with each other. Once the relationships become more established, this type of prompting should not be so necessary, but it is certainly an essential part of the coordinator's role throughout programme delivery. A three-strike rule should be implemented rigorously for the mentors or coaches to follow, ensuring that not too much time elapses before contact is made following the matching process. This should be introduced at the mentor training stage and referred to again within the support workshops if it appears to be a common issue. The rule consists of three steps that a mentor or coach should take when making initial contact with their allocated learner. Once an introductory email is sent to their learner, no more than three days should elapse before this is followed up with a reminder and a second email. If after another three days have elapsed there is still no response, then the coordinator should be contacted to follow it up.

For some programmes it will be the learner who is given the responsibility for making the first contact, and this is perfectly acceptable. In particular, where the mentors or coaches are volunteers from the business community and the learners are higher education students, this arrangement would certainly be more common. It may be in these instances that the mentors or coaches are slow to respond and so a similar three-strike rule should also apply to them, although you may feel it prudent to extend the three-day leeway in their case.

Taking these steps ensures that no more than six days are wasted before any action is taken and that coaches or mentors can be re-matched quickly in the event that their allocated learner has indeed withdrawn. The coordinator can also take any necessary action to ensure that contact details are correct, and more often than not this intervention in itself is enough to prompt a participant to respond. In some cases it is the mentor or coach who needs to be prompted in this way, but a rigorous recruitment and selection process should keep this to a minimum.

It is essential that, whatever the arrangement, the boundaries and expectations are made clear to both parties in both the training programme and in the induction process. This avoids any doubt on either side, and it will then be very apparent when the coordinator's intervention is required.

Supervision workshops should be offered at least on a monthly basis, and the coordinator should also be available to answer any urgent queries between workshops via email or phone. A plan for supervision workshops should be based upon your particular scheme and what you hope will be achieved. A good format is to allow an hour or so for group work and a second hour for individuals to drop in and have the opportunity to discuss concerns or worries on a one-to-one basis. More information on themes for support workshops can be found in Chapter 9; preparing for these and delivering them is integral to the success of your scheme.

Collecting feedback from all participants and stakeholders as well as designing data collection instruments are parts of the coordinator role that should not be overlooked. As with all good evaluation, it should not be left until the end of the programme to decide what questions will be asked of your participants. It is prudent to collect mid-way feedback, as this could enable you to make changes and alterations to improve the provision earlier rather than later. It will also bring to light any topics that might be useful to include in your support mentor or coach workshops. Inevitably a final evaluation report will be required to determine impact and to satisfy stakeholders that your objectives and targets have been met. At the very least, exploration of why targets have not been achieved should be included.

The following are guidelines for the basic requirements of the coordinator role:

▶ Identifying and recruiting suitable coaches or mentors for the programme
▶ Identifying and recruiting suitable learners for the programme
▶ Ensuring that all participants are aware that they have the right to decline the invitation to take part in the mentoring or coaching scheme or withdraw at any time
▶ Raising the awareness and understanding of other colleagues within the organisation about the mentoring or coaching scheme and outcomes

▶ Developing and delivering (or organising) appropriate mentor or coach training

▶ Inducting learners, ensuring that they are aware of their responsibilities and boundaries within the relationship

▶ Matching mentors or coaches with the learners

▶ Introducing mentors or coaches to the learners – either face to face, at an event, or through a profile swap

▶ Ensuring that appropriate accommodation is available for the sessions

▶ Providing on-going support for the mentors and coaches for the duration of the ensuing relationships

▶ Identifying and helping to resolve any issues linked to maintaining the mentoring or coaching relationship

▶ Obtaining feedback on a regular basis from both mentors/coaches and learners and other stakeholders

▶ Carrying out a complete evaluation of the scheme including mid-way feedback

This list is not exhaustive as coordinators will inevitably find that they will be sourcing additional information or resources in order to support their mentors and coaches with their individual learner issues. The following case study illustrates the need for a dedicated coordinator with sufficient time to further develop and manage the programme cleverly, using 'Lead Mentors' to assist with delivery.

CASE STUDY 1
International Student Mentoring Program (USA)

Name of institution: UC Berkeley

Name of program: International Mentorship Program

Number of years that the program has been delivered: 3 years

Number of mentors: 41 mentors plus 2 lead mentors (2015)

Number of mentees:
In 2014, 777 applications were received from incoming international freshmen and transfers. 346 of those applications were complete (anyone who submits a complete application is admitted to the program).

Who is supported:
Incoming first-year UC Berkeley international students (freshmen and transfers).

How the need was identified:
The need was identified based on 1) wanting to make small communities of support within a very large, very decentralized campus and 2) from a need assessment conducted in 2011 in which students indicated that they would like this type of community-building support.

The aims/objectives for the mentoring:
▶ To assist new students in making a successful academic and personal adjustment to UC Berkeley, thereby increasing the likelihood that they will stay through graduation
▶ To build small communities of support among first-year international students by exploring shared interests, passions, or academics
▶ To introduce and connect students to campus resources
▶ To assist students in making the most out of their college experience, including developing goals
▶ To provide current students an opportunity in which they can further their intercultural experiences, develop leadership skills, and personal and professional growth

The definition/model of mentoring that is adopted:
There are two main aims: to create a small community of friends and for the mentor to be someone that the new students feel comfortable turning to with any questions they may have. The goal is not for the mentor to have all the answers, but for them to help the student learn where to go on campus to obtain their answer – so acting as a resource. Each mentor is asked to communicate one on one with their mentees each month, and it is up to the mentor to decide how to communicate – email, text, phone call, in person meet up, etc. Mentors aim to get their small group together (each mentor has about 10 mentees) once per month, in person.

How suitable mentors are selected and recruited:
There is a two-step application process in which students are first required to fill out an application and appropriate candidates are invited to interview. Final selections are made after interviews are concluded. Students who are mature, have a passion for giving back/helping others, have increased intercultural sensitivity, and who are able – and willing – to commit and dedicate the necessary time are selected.

The duration of the mentoring relationships:
Mentors are expected to maintain contact and maintain their duties from June until November (just before Thanksgiving break). After then, the students are more focused on finals and it is difficult for them to maintain a high level of engagement through to the very end of the semester.

However, many past mentors have reported maintaining mentor/mentee and friendship relationships past this 'end date'.

The mentor training plan:
A full day of training is mandatory in April for the new mentors that covers a wide range of topics, and one professional development/check in meeting per month (Sept–Nov). There is an active Facebook group where mentors post questions to one another (and to the Coordinator and the lead mentors), as well as monthly sharing of challenges and success with one another (also online). The Coordinator delivers the full-day training and the professional development meetings are facilitated by guests from other departments on campus (counseling and psychological services, career center, etc.). Mentors are also requested to complete a survey (utilizing Survey Monkey) to gather feedback for program improvements, and to assess if the learning objective (providing current students an opportunity in which they can further their intercultural experiences, develop leadership skills, and personal and professional growth) was achieved. A manual is also provided that gives tips, guidance, suggestions, and resources that the mentors can refer to at any point.

The mentee induction process:
The mentees are required to complete an application that asks them basic demographical questions, what they are looking for in a mentor, how they preferred to be matched (based on mutual academic or extracurricular interests), why they want to be in the program, what they are most looking forward to and what they are most nervous about coming to Berkeley. Anyone who fully completes these questions is welcomed into the program. Survey Monkey is used to assess the mentees and to ensure that the program is meeting the stated learning outcomes.

Matching criteria and process:
Mentees are asked if they would like to be in a group with a mentor who shares their academic interests, or extracurricular (10 options are given). The Coordinator then tries to match each mentee to a mentor that shares their preferred interest as well as the other mentees in the group, all whilst trying to ensure the group is coming from a wide range of countries.

Frequency of the meetings:
Mentors are asked to communicate one on one with each of their mentees at least once per month, and to get their small group of mentees together monthly. An all-program-wide party is held each month. The meetings take place in a variety of locations (restaurants, campus buildings, movies, residences, etc.).

How the mentors are supported:
Monthly 'reports' that share successes or challenges where mentors identify where they need additional support or what common questions their mentees have, monthly check-in/professional development trainings, Facebook and email conversations. Mentors also reach out to the lead mentors or coordinator at any time they have any issues or questions.

The Mentoring Coordinator role:
The program has an allocated member of staff who coordinates the scheme. Hours worked by the Coordinator fluctuate depending on time of year. Some weeks are much heavier (such as during the application/interview period and the matching time) than weeks during the summer. On average this amounts to around 5 hours/week. However, significantly more time could be allocated to the role.

Funding arrangements:
There is no specific funding for the program. The events offered are free or nearly free. Partnerships with campus or local community resources help with any programmatic costs, but the mentors are all volunteers. Any events that require payment (ice skating for example) are self-funded by the students.

Evaluation arrangements :
Evaluation is conducted through assessment of the mentees and mentors (separately) to establish whether or not the learning outcomes were met. There is also an opportunity for an informal assessment of the program through the qualitative data that emerges from the hiring process. Those who are applying for a position usually disclose their past experience with the Peer Mentorship Program: whether they were in the program as mentees, and how their experience in the program motivated them to become a mentor (whether they had a positive or negative experience). Mentees in the program also have opportunities to share their experiences with me (the mentoring coordinator) via email.

Major obstacles in setting up the program:
Available time to coordinate the program is a major obstacle. The program could be a full-time job and there is much more that could be done with it if there was sufficient time. Additional time would allow for more programming elements for the mentors: a leadership development course could be implemented; more time could be given to program events for all to attend, to check in with the mentors in one-to-one meetings, and to research ways to increase mentee engagement could be prioritized given the time.

How these are overcome:

Information is shared between schools of a similar size to ensure good practice, preventing the need to reinvent the wheel. What is working, what isn't, and what is challenging are shared with one another to improve all the programs. The first year required the most time, and the subsequent years less so. Finding the time to produce high quality products (such as an eight-hour retreat and a thorough reference manual) was essential in the first year and more time was dedicated to the program during this period.

Program recommendations:

Feedback from past participants led to the implementation of one large-scale event for the entire group (all mentors and mentees) per month. Mentors requested more opportunities to connect with one another throughout the semester. Utilizing technology has resulted in increased interaction in the Facebook group, through the email listserv and Google Docs. The monthly meetings continue and co-programming with each another is encouraged. Mentors also wanted increased and frequent communication with their mentees: although the key to increasing mentee engagement is still being considered. Currently, the matching process is quite difficult due to the high numbers. Attempts are made to best connect several hundred students with a mentor who would be a 'good' fit allowing for several preference choices with the hope of providing high quality matching. However ways to reduce the amount of time needed to do so would be welcome.

3 For What Purposes Can Mentoring or Coaching Be Utilised?

As has already been seen, mentoring and coaching can be used in a variety of settings and to meet a number of different objectives. I am saddened by the number of organisations that use a mentoring or coaching programme as a means of 'ticking a box' rather than to satisfy a genuine agenda. By paying lip service to a programme, some institutions use it as a means to impress certain regulatory organisations by stating that they have a mentoring or coaching programme in place. Unfortunately, the programme may not necessarily be well organised or meet any targets, but its mere existence is sufficient to impress. This text is directed at those who have a genuine desire to use mentoring/coaching to meet their aims and objectives through a well-run programme rather than as a numbers game. As already demonstrated, this takes a serious investment of time, energy, and funding. The growing body of organisations that regulate mentoring and coaching provision, such as the Mentoring & Befriending Foundation in the UK, the ICF (International Coach Federation) in the USA, and the EMCC (European Mentoring & Coaching Council), will hopefully serve to continue to improve practice.

As mentioned previously, it would be advisable to spend some time talking to your intended beneficiaries to determine not only the precise need for support but also to establish whether coaching or mentoring might achieve that. It is essential to know exactly what it is that you hope to achieve through a mentoring or coaching intervention. To decide to introduce a mentoring or coaching programme because it sounds like a socially responsible thing to do in order to improve life at your organisation is not really sufficient reason. If you can determine exactly what aspects of life at the organisation you would like to improve, then you will be better able to measure any outcomes.

Many higher education institutions now deliver outreach programmes to support pupils in local schools for a variety of reasons. Delivered properly, pupil mentoring can have an extremely beneficial impact on both the pupils and the undergraduate mentors. Specific information on school-based mentoring is covered in Chapter 12.

Although the list of possible aims and objectives is endless, some of the more common ones are listed below.

▶ Higher education student support

- ▶ To raise attainment in a specific programme of study using more experienced peers as mentors or coaches
- ▶ To raise attainment in a specific programme of study using staff as mentors/coaches
- ▶ To improve student retention rates either generally or for specific courses/programmes of study
- ▶ To narrow the attainment gap of specific groups of students (such as students from lower socioeconomic groups or some ethnic minority students)
- ▶ To support international students, particularly if they are studying in a country where the language is different from their own native language
- ▶ To support students with the transition to work and with career choices using external mentors or coaches
- ▶ To support students with the transition to work and with career choices using alumni
- ▶ To support those currently studying at foundation/vocational degree level encouraging them to continue with their education
- ▶ Using postgraduate students in their final year/s (or staff) to support those who are embarking on postgraduate study

▶ School Pupil Support

Using higher education students as mentors or coaches to support children in the following areas:

- ▶ To raise the educational aspirations of children who come from families who have no tradition of applying for higher education courses
- ▶ To raise the attainment of young people who are underperforming in specific subject areas
- ▶ To increase the number of female or male students applying for either male-dominated or female-dominated courses
- ▶ To support pupils who have emotional behavioural difficulties or who are in danger of being excluded from mainstream education
- ▶ To support school pupils who have emigrated to a different culture and education system to help with integration and possible language barriers perhaps using bilingual mentors or coaches

▶ Mentoring transition provided by undergraduates to support pupils who are moving from junior to senior school
▶ To support children who are in 'government' or 'public' care or fostered

▶ Miscellaneous examples of support programmes

▶ Technology mentoring whereby higher education students support academic staff with assistive teaching technologies
▶ Apprenticeship mentoring with volunteers encouraging those in a workplace environment who have not as yet embarked on any form of higher education to do so
▶ Single mothers mentoring whereby those who are struggling to cope with the demands of study, work and being a parent are supported by others who have overcome similar barriers
▶ Support for mature learners who may be in the minority within their peer group and who may have more unusual challenges than their peers (such as balancing the demands of employment with study)

In addition to the above suggestions you may wish to develop a staff-to-staff mentoring or coaching programme. This could be for staff who are new to the institution or for those who are new to a management role. Your mentors or coaches in these cases could be more experienced or senior staff, or a cross-institutional coaching or mentoring programme could be investigated.

▶ The targeted group

Before embarking on your programme and having identified the need and anticipated the desired outcome, you will still need to consider whether working with the identified group is actually feasible. They may be extremely hard to reach and potentially impossible to engage with, despite your best efforts. This difficulty was encountered in the case of pupils who were either at risk of being or had already been excluded from mainstream school as well as higher education students who had been parented in the 'social care system' (or 'care-leavers' as they are known in the UK). Although these individuals could potentially benefit from the support of a mentor or coach, they are unlikely to be very willing to identify themselves and put themselves forward. There may be a number of reasons for this, such as not wanting to differentiate themselves from their peers, not wanting to appear 'uncool', or just being distrustful of one-to-one close relationships. Whatever the reason, careful promotion of the programme will be required, and skilfully conducted introductory sessions will be necessary. A very successful programme for 'excluded' young people was delivered at my own institution, and the identified pupils were invited to an introductory session to hear about the mentoring. The trained undergraduate mentors also attended, and some creative and fun activities were delivered whereby the mentors and the pupils worked in teams and so got to know each other a little. The activities consisted of things such as building towers with uncooked spaghetti and marshmallows to see which team could build the highest tower, with the youngest member of the team being in charge. To ensure that every mentor had the chance to engage, even if for a short while, with each of the pupils, a speed matching activity was also conducted. This is simply where two rows of seats are laid out, face to face, one with mentors seated and the other with pupils. They are then given 60 seconds to find out a fact or two about the person sitting in front of them, until an alarm is sounded when the mentors have to move onto the next person, until they arrive back in their starting position. In between these activities the pupils are informed about the mentoring; and it is explained to them how it works in practice (i.e. they will meet with their mentors once a week; and they are also told that they can opt out). Once the activities are over, each pupil is taken aside and asked firstly if they are interested in working with any of the mentors. If so they are then asked if there were any with whom they would not wish to work or if they can give the names of one or two with whom they would be happy to work. This choice being given, it is very rare in my experience for the pupils to decline the opportunity of working with one of the mentors. Obviously it is essential that the mentors are all suitably experienced, friendly and approachable. Likewise in my experience, using this approach has never left any one mentor un-selected by the pupils. This method also has the bonus of allowing the pupils to choose whom they work with, which automatically sets the relationship off to a good start.

This type of method can be successfully adapted for adults, although the activities delivered will perhaps need to be made more age appropriate. The 'speed matching' however is always a winner, whether it is children or adults who are taking part.

For other hard-to-reach groups some imagination may be required to ensure that you can gather them together. It may be possible to utilise some other event that they will be attending anyway and take the opportunity of addressing them at the end or beginning of this. Other alternatives might be to have some good promotional materials. These can be handed out to those in your group by other individuals (such as programme tutors) who are scheduled to meet with them anyway, so that they can alert them to the opportunity. This highlights the need to ensure that others within your institution are both aware and supportive of your programme.

If you have concerns that your intended group might be hard to reach, then it may be prudent to promote the opportunity first, asking for expressions of interest before fully embarking on the implementation. It may also be that you are made aware of the need for support by another agency. The case study below demonstrates how the need for peer mentoring was initially identified through different departments within the university and then piloted.

CASE STUDY 2
Disability Mentoring Programme (UK)

Name of institution: SE University

Name of programme: Peer Mentoring

Number of years that the programme has been delivered: Since 2006

Number of mentors: 8 in 2006 rising to 18 in 2008

Number of mentees:
2006 – 10 matches
2007 – 16 matches
2008 – 18 matches
2009 – onwards 25 + (but now delivered by paid external mentors)

Who is supported:
Any students who have a physical disability, mental health issue, or an SpLD (specific learning difference) such as dyslexia.

How the need was identified:
Peer mentoring had been available for some time within the institution but consisted solely of using undergraduates as mentors to support school pupils who faced barriers.

From discussions with the counselling service, the Mentoring Team, and Student Support professionals (such as house wardens) it became apparent that a number of students might benefit from the support of a peer rather than a professional. The counselling service was seeing an increasing number of students who reportedly felt lonely and were finding it difficult to integrate into university life. The students also reported that they were finding the workload stressful and were not managing their time very well. The Counselling Service was finding it difficult to meet the needs of these students with the limited resources available. House wardens too had reported difficulties for students with disabilities such as Asperger's Syndrome or mental health issues. It was thought by the counsellors particularly that many of these students might benefit more from a well-trained peer mentor than from a counsellor to help with the integration and isolation issues. A proportion of these students did have a disability or mental health issue that was being monitored by the mental health team, and hence the Disability Peer mentoring programme was conceived.

The aims/objectives for the mentoring:
The objective for the mentoring was to help integrate the students into university life so that they could make the most of the opportunities available to them both socially and academically. The programme also strove to ensure that the students accessed the various other forms of professional support available to them as required.

The definition/model of mentoring that was adopted:
The face-to-face sessions are all conducted on a one-to-one basis, and the mentors are trained to be facilitative rather than directive. They are trained not to give advice but to ask open questions and explore options.

How suitable mentors are selected and recruited:
Undergraduates in the pilot scheme were initially invited to apply for the role of mentor through short recruitment talks given at lectures or induction sessions. The promotional materials suggested that for the role it would be useful to have direct experience of disability and/or overcoming such barriers. Mentors are selected via a process of application form and interview. Two interviewers score each participant with a minimum requirement to be accepted onto the programme. Attributes sought include good listening skills and an empathetic attitude as well as a good understanding of the issues faced.

The duration of the mentoring relationships:
A maximum of a whole academic year.

The mentor training plan:
There is a two-day training programme delivered by the mentoring and coaching team. It includes exploring the role of a mentor, communications skills, action planning/target setting, and the application of mentoring tools designed specifically to improve social integration. There is a short assessment that asks the students to respond to a case study scenario and suggest how they might deal with it. It is assessed by the mentoring and coaching team using set criteria to judge their questioning skills, action planning/goal setting and appropriate use of mentoring tools. Successful completion of this assessment is essential for inclusion in

the programme. Included in the training plan is a session delivered by the Disability Officer on particular disabilities and the impact that these may have on student life.

The mentee induction process:
The programme is promoted through the intranet and student support/counselling services and by tutors. Every student who wishes to apply for a mentor is required to complete an application form and attend an individual induction session with the scheme coordinator. The induction process informs them of their responsibilities and of the boundaries of the mentoring relationship. There is also discussion about the available mentors, and the students are given a choice of whom they would prefer to work with.

Matching criteria and process:
Initial discussions take place with the mentee who makes the choice although the coordinator can recommend a particular mentor who they feel may be suitable. The selected mentor is then approached to check that he or she feels comfortable with the match. Once agreement is obtained, the mentor and mentee are introduced by the coordinator at a joint meeting. Alternatively the mentor is provided with the contact details of the mentee and makes the first approach.

Frequency of the meetings:
A guideline of one meeting per week for an hour's duration is used, although many choose to communicate regularly via text and phone as well.

How the mentors are supported:
The mentors are required, as part of their commitment, to attend support workshops at least once per month. These are a forum in which to meet fellow mentors and discuss ideas and experiences, and they are offered throughout the programme. In addition to this an allocated coordinator is available by phone or email to offer advice and support for issues that are of a more urgent nature.

The coordinator role:
The programme has an assigned coordinator who works on an equivalent 0.5 FTE basis. However the hours fluctuate from a near full-time post at the beginning of the programme to becoming less intensive once the matching process is completed. The hours worked increase again at the end of the programme when the evaluation and data collection take place.

Funding arrangements:
The programme was originally funded jointly by the Counselling Service and Student Support. No payment, apart from vouchers, was given to

the student mentors. Since 2009 however the scheme has been funded using Disabled Student Allowance for the identified students as part of their support package. The mentors are no longer peers but external and paid an hourly rate.

Evaluation arrangements:

Evaluation is conducted through pre and post questionnaires. A series of questions is asked to establish the mentees' satisfaction with student life both before and after the mentoring. They are also given the opportunity to provide qualitative feedback and suggestions for improvement to the programme. Feedback is also sought from the mentors and tutors. The evaluation reports are shared with the other departments within the university.

Overcoming obstacles within the programme:

Initially mentor applications were relatively low as it was specified that the mentors should themselves have a disability. The criterion was extended to include those who had experience of disability either through friends or family or work (including volunteering). This resulted in increased applications, and it also became apparent that for some disabilities, matching people with a similar disability would not result in an appropriate match. For example, matching a visually impaired mentor with a visually impaired mentee or matching a mentee and mentor who both have Asperger's Syndrome may not always be suitable.

In the pilot scheme extensive training was delivered to the mentors on several different disabilities and the impact that these might have. It was found quite quickly that not all disabilities could be covered in the training and that the mentees who applied often had a disability that had not been covered in the session. In these cases, if appropriate, the mentor could be briefed individually prior to being matched. Subsequently the 'disability training session' became far more general and aimed to ensure that the mentors were taught to have a general awareness of how a disability might impact but not to patronise their allocated mentees.

It also became apparent that not all matches were immediately obvious. One mentor had a teenage daughter with dyslexia and it was initially assumed that she would be an ideal candidate to work with a learner who had dyslexia. However the mentor felt that she had 'exhausted her reserves' with dyslexia support in her personal life and she preferred to support a learner with a different issue. Another mentor felt unable to support anyone who was being treated for cancer. Someone close in her family had undergone cancer treatment and she felt that it would be too personal an issue and evoke too many painful memories. In view of such experiences the mentors were subsequently asked to specify any issues that they would not be comfortable working with to prevent a mismatch.

Programme recommendations:

Ideally both professional and peer mentors should be offered, as many students prefer support from a peer rather than a 'professional'.

Even with a well-organised programme, you will often find that applications are slow to begin with, but they will gain momentum as more people hear about it. It is wise not to set your targets too high at the start and to expand the provision slowly as the demand grows.

▶ Who will be the mentors or coaches?

Once it has been established exactly what you hope to achieve by your mentoring or coaching programme, the next step is to decide which is the best placed group of people who could be trained to offer the support. Some compromise may be necessary here as there are a number of factors to consider in this decision such as:

Geography

Questions to consider are:

- ▶ *Will face-to-face meetings be feasible for your coaches or mentors?*
- ▶ *If not, will ementoring be a possibility?*
- ▶ *Are any of the participants likely to have mobility or transport issues impacting on possible meetings?*
- ▶ *What budget is there, if any, to pay participants to travel to meetings?*
- ▶ *If your mentors are geographically widespread, how will you train them?*

It may be that the best mentors or coaches to suit the needs of your scheme are not local, in which case it might be better to implement an ementoring programme and develop an online training programme. If they have to travel to have face-to-face meetings, this will need to be accounted for in your allocated budget. Ementoring will allow contact if your participants are geographically widespread, but generally people prefer to have at least one face-to-face meeting. These decisions will also depend on your individual mentors or coaches and learners. They will need to be familiar with the use of these methods of communication for them to work effectively. Video calls and conferencing are now also quite commonplace and can be utilised as part of the mentoring process.

Knowledge and Experience

Questions to consider are:

▶ How much knowledge of the 'topic' is it necessary for your mentors or coaches to have?
▶ If the mentors or coaches will not have much prior knowledge of the topic, what other resources or information sources will be available for them?
▶ How can (and how much of) the information that they might need be included in the training programme?
▶ How much experience and knowledge will they need to have in order to be credible to your potential learners?

Your mentors or coaches do need to be credible to your learners as they will be likely to remain un-selected if not. However they do not need to have a huge existing knowledge of the topic or theme of the programme especially if this information is readily available to them throughout. For example, you may have a mentor who has worked in the field of engineering for many years in the same organisation as part of your 'career mentoring programme' who has an excellent knowledge of the requirements to work in this industry. However, it may be some time since he or she wrote a CV or applied for jobs and he or she may therefore have a limited knowledge of other engineering organisations. It would be wise to utilise such mentors as part of your programme, and the gaps in their knowledge can be easily filled should the need arise. They should be made aware, as part of the training, that CV formats constantly evolve and that, should they need to support their allocated learners in this respect, they should be informed of where to access the appropriate resources. This information could even be provided in the handbook and training materials.

A lesson about how to utilise time more effectively was learned in an attempt to teach mentors about the different disabilities that they might encounter with their potential learners in a Disability Mentoring programme. The case study on page 25 shows how the programme evolved. Training time was invested unnecessarily during the training in covering a range of disabilities and how they might present a barrier to learning. In reality there were applications from learners with more uncommon disabilities that had not been covered as part of the training.

It became apparent quite quickly that there was little point in delivering the training in this way and subsequently each mentor was given information about the specific disability of their allocated mentee (if they needed it) prior to being matched. This was a much more time-efficient means of preparing the mentors for their role.

A similar concept was utilised when developing a technology mentoring programme. Rather than training every mentor in every technology (which was costly both in terms of time and funding) technology mentors underwent training in specific technological areas as and when required.

It must always be remembered that a certain amount of background knowledge in a subject area, whether that is industry based or in specific higher education courses, will be essential in order for the coach or mentor to be an attractive prospect for the learner to work with. This is especially so if it is intended for your learners to select the mentor or coach of their choice as part of the matching process.

Expertise

Questions to consider are:

▶ *How much expertise in the particular context is necessary in order for your mentors or coaches to support the learners?*
▶ *Will too much expertise result in the coaches or mentors being too directive and being pre-judgemental?*
▶ *Will expertise in one specific area prohibit them from supporting in a wider range of topics?*

How much expertise is required in a particular area is another decision that needs to be taken into account. In some respects being an 'expert' in a specific field will perhaps reduce the breadth of the support offered to the learner. In some cases too much expertise can lead to the mentor or coach being too directive and making presumptions about what is best for their learner. Careful training is essential to prevent this from occurring.

There have been instances whereby the coach or mentor considered him- or herself an expert on a particular topic and had the expectation of only helping in that precise area. However, the reality is that other issues may emerge as part of the sessions. For example a coaching programme was implemented to support higher education students who were not achieving well academically. It turned out that a number of students who applied for the support had other more personal issues that had been distracting them from their studies and these emerged during the course of their coaching sessions. Some of the coaches found the discussion of more personal issues challenging, and this is where the support workshops can be very useful in helping the coaches or mentors to manage these situations. It would not have been advisable to force coaches to deal with these more personal issues if they really did not feel able to. In most cases with support from the coordinator and reassurance they were able to meet these expectations despite it being an unexpected responsibility for them. It also expanded their skill development as coaches. In other cases the coaches were supported in encouraging their learners to seek support for the more personal issues elsewhere, such as from friends, family, the mental health well-being officer or the counselling service. This is where the coordinator role is so important in gauging the optimum outcome for the individual circumstances and bringing these situations to a mutually satisfactory conclusion.

These types of circumstances can be avoided to some degree by setting very clear guidelines and boundaries at the outset for the learners. Some of your mentors or coaches may feel comfortable with conversation of a more personal nature. If this is the case, another way to avoid a mismatch is for the coach or mentor to allude to this in their 'profile'. The content of a 'profile' will be discussed in Chapter 7. The profile should be a good indicator of the strengths and characteristics of each coach so that the learner is more aware of what is acceptable, or not, for each of the individual coaches or mentors.

The training process should also identify those coaches and mentors who will likely have a broader or narrower remit in the support they feel they can offer. This information will help in the matching process. Monitoring at the training will also allow the coordinator to identify any potential issues with the matching process. An example of this is where one peer mentor had strong views, due to religious beliefs, regarding homosexuality and expressed a concern about being matched with anyone who was openly homosexual. This was a somewhat contentious issue which needed open and honest discussion. In a disability mentoring programme, one mentor felt unable to support anyone who was being treated for cancer because of her personal experiences as can be seen from the case study on page 25. Another mentor, a mother of a teenage daughter with dyslexia, was not keen to support a student with dyslexia as she felt that she exhausted her reserves on this topic.

These examples demonstrate that expertise in a specific area is not necessarily good or useful. It also shows the individuality of people and how important it is for coordinators to work closely with their mentors and coaches to know what is and isn't a good match.

Practical Elements

Questions to consider are:

▶ *Will the intended mentors or coaches have sufficient time to commit to your programme?*
▶ *Will taking part in the programme have any unfavourable effects on your mentors or coaches?*
▶ *What will be the benefits for your mentors or coaches and will these attract sufficient numbers to apply?*
▶ *Will your intended mentors or coaches have the approval of their line manager, tutors, etc. to take part?*
▶ *What age are your intended mentors or coaches and will this likely meet the needs and expectations of the learners?*
▶ *Will the mentors and coaches (and the learners) have access to suitable technology to enable other forms of contact such as 'Skype' or 'Facetime' if face-to-face meetings are not possible?*

These factors can be extremely significant. Whilst there may be a group of people who are obviously eminently suitable for the role it may be that they would not have sufficient time or support to take part in your programme. Many an eager volunteer has subsequently been reminded by their line manager or programme tutor that they are unlikely to have the time to spare, instilling doubt that they would be able to cope with the demands of the role. This point may or may not be justified and arguably the cost in time may well be outweighed by the other benefits of taking part. Many coaches and mentors have reported an improved understanding of the subject in hand or the embedding of knowledge by helping someone else, which has in turn improved their own performance. This is why part of the coordinator's role is to ensure that others within the organisation are aware and supportive of the programme so that they can then support you in encouraging people to take part.

However, it may be the case that there is viably no time available for your selected group to take part in face-to-face sessions. This could be circumvented by ementoring or other forms of contact if that were possible although it will still require a commitment of a certain amount of their time. It will be seen in Chapter 11 that ementoring can be utilised in certain contexts very usefully but is not always the best option when the exchanges are anticipated to be more than functional. If ementoring is decided upon, then it will be essential that your mentors or coaches have the technological skills and access to the intended medium.

Age is another quite crucial factor. Most learners are not overly keen to work with someone who is younger than them, even if she or he does have more experience. Equally, too much of an age gap can also be a barrier. Sometimes a large age gap can bring with it a lack of empathetic understanding of a situation, although not always. Industry and trends do change quite rapidly, which is why it is so important that a mentor or coach listens closely to the views and opinions of their learner and makes no assumptions about their situation.

It may in some cases be preferable to choose a group of people who have less experience to be your coaches rather than those who have an abundance of experience but no real time to spare. Of course there is always the possibility of utilising some from each of your identified groups, particularly if it is a pilot scheme enabling you to monitor which of the participants fare better.

Anticipated numbers

Questions to consider are:

▶ Are you likely to be able to recruit sufficient numbers of coaches or mentors to meet the anticipated needs?
▶ If not, then what other resource pools might be available to select from?
▶ What might incentivise more people to apply to be a mentor or coach?
▶ What is in it for them, how will they benefit?
▶ How many learners can you expect each coach or mentor to work with?

It will be essential to determine the size of your mentoring or coaching scheme from the beginning and adhere to that. If you receive more applications to be a coach or mentor than targeted, then you will have a selection process and criteria in place to ensure that only the best are chosen. What is more usual, however, is to be short in volunteer numbers, but do not be tempted to accept unsuitable applicants in order to meet your target. It would be better to identify another group of people to ask. For example in an academic peer coaching programme an unexpected number of final year students applied for support and there were too few post graduate students to match them with. As a result the invitation to take part as a coach was extended to members of staff in order to satisfy demand.

Changes may have to be made to the intended provision to make the programme more attractive or realistic. It may be that you had set the duration of the mentoring to be for a whole academic year. However for some potential mentors or coaches this commitment may be too long, and so reducing the commitment to one semester only may result in increased applications.

Depending on the available time of your coaches or mentors, it may be that you can increase the ratio of coaches or mentors to learners. Perhaps some of your coaches or mentors will be able to support two or more learners. Care must be taken, however, not to over-burden them so as to be detrimental to their own studies or work. Sometimes well-intentioned and eager mentors are too enthusiastic about taking on more learners. As a coordinator you too will be eager to match your learners with a suitably enthusiastic coach or mentor but if subsequently it becomes too time consuming they may withdraw from the programme completely. As a coordinator you should be very cautious about this and not be persuaded by an urgent need to match a learner as it could have calamitous consequences.

Other ways of increasing the number of applicants may be to offer an incentive although large monetary ones should be avoided for fear of attracting applicants for the wrong reason. Incentives can be varied and range from certification or accreditation for their efforts to vouchers or book tokens. At this stage it is worth checking your promotional material to ensure that the benefits for the mentors and coaches are clearly defined and appropriate. For example a personal reference will be invaluable for an undergraduate with no work experience but of little use to someone who has been in employment for a number of years.

The following case study demonstrates how despite best efforts and good practice in mentor recruitment and training, the size and scale of the programme became unmanageable. Combined with an attempt to make the mentoring mandatory for mentees, it was untenable.

CASE STUDY 3
Large-Scale Undergradute Mentoring Programme (UK)

Name of institution: SE University

Name of programme: Peer Mentoring

Number of years that the programme has been delivered: Since 2012

Number of mentors: 2014 – 450

Number of mentees:
250 in 2012
850 in 2013
1,450 in 2014

Who is supported:
HE students who are identified as widening participation students/from lower socioeconomic groups

How the need was identified:
Mentoring had successfully been established within the University to support students who faced barriers such as a disability or mental health issues and for school pupils. With the introduction of Government

National Scholarship funding it was decided to utilise some of this funding to offer mentoring support to the students who had been identified as being from a lower socioeconomic group as well as being the first in the family to embark on HE study.

The aims/objectives for the mentoring:
The aim of the mentoring was to encourage social integration, aid retention and improve student satisfaction scores.

The definition/model of mentoring that was adopted:
The contact consists of one-to-one, face-to-face meetings with the addition of e-mentoring, Skype, or texting between sessions.

The model of mentoring is based on best practice and is nondirective, empowering the mentees to make their own decisions and take advantage of the opportunities offered at the university.

How suitable mentors are selected and recruited:
Undergraduates are invited to apply for the role of mentor through short recruitment talks given at lectures or induction sessions. Mentors are selected via a process of application form and interview. Two interviewers score each participant with a minimum requirement in order for them to be accepted onto the programme.

The duration of the mentoring relationships:
One academic year commencing September/October

The mentor training plan:
There is a two-day training programme delivered by the mentoring team. It includes an exploration of the role of a mentor, communications skills, action planning/target setting, and the application of mentoring tools. There is a short assessment that asks the students to respond to a case study scenario and suggest how they might deal with it. It is assessed by the mentoring team using set criteria to judge their questioning skills, action planning/goal setting and appropriate use of coaching tools. Successful completion of this assessment is essential for inclusion in the programme.

The mentee induction process:
The mentees are informed by letter/email that they will be offered a mentor and are invited to book on to a group induction session. They are given a presentation by the Mentoring Coordinator to explain the aims and objectives of the programme, what to expect from their allocated mentor and how to make best use of the opportunity. They complete a pre-questionnaire to establish what they might like support with. During the induction the mentees are shown the profiles of the mentors and

asked to indicate their preference for three of them. They are informed that they can opt out of the programme if they wish.

Matching criteria and process:
The pre-questionnaire from both the mentor and the mentee are used to make best matches where possible but the choice is also dictated by the mentee's stated preferences.

Frequency of the meetings:
A guideline is given of one meeting per week or fortnight for an hour's duration or according to the needs of the mentee and mentor availability.

How the mentors are supported:
The mentors are required, as part of their commitment, to attend support workshops at least once per month. These are a forum in which to meet fellow mentors and to discuss ideas and experiences. They are offered fortnightly throughout the programme. In addition to this an allocated coordinator is available by phone or email to offer advice and support for issues that are of a more urgent nature. Additional training/support is also offered as part of the workshops on specific common issues such as mentees not responding to emails or failing to turn up to arranged meetings.

The Mentoring Coordinator role:
The programme has designated mentoring coordinators who work the equivalent of 4 X FTE plus a full-time administrator.

Funding arrangements:
The programme is funded by the Government's National Scholarship Programme.

Evaluation arrangements:
Evaluation is conducted through pre and post questionnaires. A series of questions is asked to establish attitudes towards higher education using a Likert scale so that progress can be measured. In the post questionnaire, mentees are also asked to identify the most useful and least useful aspects of the mentoring. They are also given the opportunity to provide qualitative feedback and suggestions for improvement. Feedback is also sought from the mentors.

Major obstacles in setting up the programme:
- In the first year, the scheme was introduced as mandatory and as such not well received by the mentees.
- The numbers of participants involved made monitoring of the relationships difficult.

► Recruiting such large numbers of mentors inevitably resulted in lowering the criteria for acceptance onto the programme.

How these are overcome:

► In subsequent years the programme has been introduced as 'standard provision' and the option to 'opt out' given earlier. This has resulted in lower numbers of matches but better quality of mentoring relationships.

► The student mentors were each allocated a specific coordinator to be their point of contact so as to maintain a more personal relationship and mechanism for support.

► A decision was taken to maintain the higher level of acceptance criteria rather than compromise on mentor quality.

Programme recommendations:

It became apparent that a mentoring programme should never be made mandatory for the mentees (or the mentors) despite the evidence to suggest that mentoring can be extremely beneficial. Despite the efforts made to maintain a more personal approach when training, supporting, and matching, it became clear that it was impossible to achieve this with such a high volume of participants. The high volume also caused issues with the matching process, and few of the mentees were allocated the mentor of their choice. This also caused negative feelings resulting in non-engagement by the mentees and frustration on behalf of the mentors who found that the mentees were not responding to them.

Despite peer support being hugely successful elsewhere within the university, it was apparent that the provision was not suitable for delivery on such a large scale. It is now only offered to a smaller number of students who request it.

4 Planning Your Programme

Delivering a robust mentoring or coaching programme is a commitment in time and there will also be some costs attached which will need to be accounted for. As was seen in Table 2.1 in Chapter 2 there are several coordinator hours to be included at whatever rate they will be paid. It is quite common to have two coordinators to share the workload, particularly if they are developing the scheme in addition to their usual posts, but these hours should always be allowed for in your calculations. Having two coordinators may increase the total hours required as they will need to liaise quite frequently to keep abreast of the pairings and developing relationships. It is also likely that both should be a part of the training process in order to familiarise themselves with their mentors or coaches. If a particularly large programme is envisaged, then the responsibilities can be divided up between them. One coordinator could be responsible for matching and induction of learners whilst the other delivers the support workshops and chases up any flagging relationships. Obviously the split will depend on the available time each has to spend on the coaching and mentoring programme or perhaps to fit in with any other work commitments.

In addition to coordinator costs an allowance will need to be made for resources such as training materials. No matter how comprehensive the training, it is best for each of your mentors and coaches to be given a handbook at the end of the training days as a reminder. Much knowledge is imparted during the training, and because it is mainly theoretical it will not be fully absorbed until your coaches and mentors actually start to work with their learners. Handbooks allow your coaches and mentors to refer back to the theory long after the training has finished.

Another resource that is wise to provide is a mentoring or coaching contact log book in which they record the gist of their sessions. Even better, a learning log could be provided that allows them to reflect on each of their sessions to further develop their skills. This will be particularly useful if you are considering offering any form of accreditation, as your mentors and coaches will need to regularly reflect on their own practice and identify areas for further development. More details on the content for these logs can be found in Chapter 8.

A mentoring or coaching toolkit is also a good addition to their pack and this will comprise of useful activities specifically designed for the remit of the project. The possible content of all these items will be explored more fully in the training, Chapter 6.

Obviously these resources can be elaborately or as simply reproduced as you wish, which in turn will dictate the costs. The presentation is not as important as the content, although poorly reproduced resources will not inspire confidence in your mentors or coaches, particularly if they are external to your institution or from the business community. Ultimately, available funding will be the prohibitive factor here.

The resources required to deliver the training programme can be relatively low cost and consist of no more than flipcharts, marker pens, and some activity sort cards and scenarios that can be created with minimal effort. The training materials too will be explored more fully in Chapter 6.

Miscellaneous additional costs such as for training room venues and refreshments, if you are providing them, plus travel expenses will also need to be accounted for. If your programme involves work with children or vulnerable people, then costs for police checks will also need to be included. Some calculations will need to be made about whether there is any possibility of reimbursing your coaches and mentors for their time. Whilst you do not want the rate of pay to be so high that it attracts people for the wrong reasons, it is nice to give some form of reward as a gratuity. It is wise however to pay this upon successful completion of the whole programme rather than as an hourly rate. You would want to discourage people from attending the training but then withdrawing without having been matched up with any of your learners.

The gratuity, if any, will also depend on from where you recruit your mentors and coaches. Higher education students very often are appreciative of any cash payment and in my experience welcome a bursary or cash payment to cover expenses at the conclusion of the programme. As this is not an hourly rate of pay it is non-taxable, but each institution will have different mechanisms in place for paying their students. For external business mentors or coaches what has been found to be more appropriate is to give vouchers. These can be online vouchers or tokens which most people will appreciate. A cash payment for these external mentors or coaches will likely prove more difficult to process and is probably not as important as it might be for students. University staff who train or volunteer for your programme can also be rewarded in this way should you wish. Of course there is no obligation to give anything at all, and you are still likely to recruit good volunteers even if you decide not to offer any monetary reward. Interestingly many bursary payments have remained uncollected in my own institution despite several email reminders. Many students express surprise when offered them, having forgotten that they were promised. They have frequently been heard to state that they would gladly have taken part for nothing as it was such an enjoyable and rewarding experience.

In the quest for fairness I would suggest creating a formula for mentor or coach payment based upon available funding. Once it is known how much is available for this purpose, a method of calculating individual bursaries can be used. This should be based upon attendance at the training sessions and support workshops, the number of meetings or exchanges that they had with their learner and, if appropriate, the number of emails that they exchanged. Using this method ensures that the payments are fairly and accurately calculated according to commitment of each individual mentor or coach. Some mentors or coaches may have worked with three or more learners and met with them weekly for a number of weeks, whilst others may have only had one learner whom they met on just three occasions. Having a formula of this type ensures that the payments are not only justifiable but fair. It also ensures that in the case of a coach or mentor having taken the trouble to undergo the training but not consequently matched up with anyone (usually through no fault of their own), they will still receive a small gratuity as a token of appreciation. This will encourage them to volunteer again when the programme is repeated when they hopefully will be matched.

Another cost that may be applicable is for an ementoring licence should you need one. As will be seen in Chapter 11 these can be extremely useful, and where you are working with school pupils it will almost certainly be essential for child protection purposes. There are a number of these platforms available, all with different facilities, and the costs vary enormously. Some exploratory work will need to be carried out to identify the most appropriate one for your programme.

You may wish to include a cost in your calculations for accreditation or certification purposes. Again this is something that will vary from institution to institution depending on what is available. It may be that some higher education credit points can be awarded in return for the commitment, or it may just consist of a simple certificate stating the skills that the individual has acquired. If the latter is to be the case, then the costs should be minimal but it is something that many higher education students will find invaluable, particularly when seeking employment. It may be that the reward for some external mentors or coaches is to receive a form of recognised accreditation in Coaching or Mentoring. This could be far more valuable to them than a voucher or a small sum of money. It may also be feasible to offer your mentors or coaches the choice of the accreditation or a bursary payment.

Other costs will include any promotional materials for either mentor or coach recruitment or to attract your targeted group to apply. These may range from flyers (which can be as simple or as elaborate as you wish) to having recruitment stands at specific events which may incur greater costs. Strategically placed posters may also be considered, and again the costs for these will vary depending on your institution and available resources.

▶ Sourcing Funding

It would be difficult in this text to direct the reader to sources of funding as this will vary not only from institution to institution but from country to country. What can be achieved however is to define the different sources of funding that have been utilised for the case study examples, allowing readers to establish what might be feasible for their particular programme. Sources of government funding are constantly changing as different target groups evolve or specific needs emerge. In 2008 to 2011 for example, in the UK significant sums of money were available to deliver programmes for school pupils from lower socioeconomic backgrounds to encourage them to apply for higher education courses. A number of highly successful mentoring programmes were delivered that had a proven effect on pupils as could be seen from the increased applications to university. However a change of government resulted in this funding being withdrawn. Schools during this period had participated in this intervention without any charge being made. After 2011 the same programmes were offered to the schools but a charge had to be made to cover the costs on a nonprofit-making basis. Many of these schools, having seen the benefits for their pupils, opted to pay the costs from their own funding, and many of the mentoring schemes continue to be delivered in this way today. To attract funding, very often it will be essential to demonstrate outcomes, making thorough evaluation of any pilot programme crucial.

A peer coaching programme within my own institution was initially piloted as a result of convincing two different academic schools of the virtues of coaching. Each contributed a small amount of funding to pilot the programme with just ten coaches from each academic school. Four years later, significant results from the two original schools having been demonstrated, five additional academic schools now contribute to the costs of this now large-scale programme supporting nearly two hundred higher education students each year. As each new academic school opted to participate, the cost per school reduced due to economies of scale. Obviously it was essential to demonstrate impact such as academic improvement of students as well as retention or improved student satisfaction results in order to attract and maintain the funding. By demonstrating that undergraduates who were initially at risk of leaving prematurely had continued with their studies as a result of the coaching, a viable case could be made for the cost effectiveness of the programme. The case study for this programme can be found on page 119.

Piloting a scheme using funding from a charitable trust is also an option and well worth investigating, especially if it can be developed into something more sustainable as has been shown above. Subscriptions to these funding-stream bulletins is usually available for a small fee in most countries and they could result in significant amounts of funding being awarded, though the time invested in writing the proposals can be quite significant.

If seeking funding for school-based mentoring programmes, then local business may be interested in investing as part of their corporate social responsibility. The recompense that would likely need to be given for this type of contribution is to include the organisational logo on all your programme materials. This is probably a small price to pay for a worthwhile programme that might significantly change the lives of many children or young people.

It is always prudent to be continually searching for new funding streams and to work collaboratively wherever possible to keep costs to a minimum. If you have a neighbouring institution reasonably close to you, then it may be feasible to develop a cross-institutional coaching or mentoring programme that may be particularly useful for staff members.

Networking with others in a similar role is always to be recommended, particularly for sourcing funding, and so these opportunities should be taken up as often as possible. In the UK a Higher Education Mentoring Managers group hosts online discussions and convenes regularly to showcase best practice and share ideas. If there is currently nothing like this available locally to you, then it might be worth considering setting something up yourself.

▶ **Timeframes**

The final word on planning your programme is on the topic of timescales. Whilst it is good to be ambitious and set yourself challenging targets, you will need to remain realistic. Very often you will be depending on others, and things do not always progress according to plan. A contingency plan is also always sensible to have for instances such as when insufficient coach or mentor applications are received or for when the number of learners seeking support is lower than anticipated.

A rough guideline process for the timescales involved will depend on the size and scale of your project, but it should follow a pattern similar to the one below. Obviously the size of the project will determine the time spent on each task. Table 4.1 below would be an approximation of the timescales for a small to medium-sized programme of 20 mentors or coaches support-ing up to 40 learners. With larger numbers it would be expected that more than one set of training dates would be arranged and a longer period of time to conduct coach or mentor interviews, thereby expanding your timescales. Too long a gap between the end of the training and being matched may lead to frustration and a waning of enthusiasm for your mentors or coaches so should be avoided. Similarly your learners should be matched as quickly as possible after the induction process.

Table 4.1 Timeframe for Setting Up and Implementing a Coaching or Mentoring Programme

Task	Timeframe
▶ Set the aims/objectives of the programme ▶ Decide on the optimum time to offer the support	Week 1–2
▶ Liaise with stakeholders to promote programme and obtain permission/funding	Week 3–4
▶ Plan and set dates for coach/mentor training ▶ Write coach/mentor recruitment material	Week 4–5
▶ Circulate promotional materials ▶ Commence mentor/coach recruitment	Week 6–7
▶ Conduct coach/mentor interviews (and police checks if required)	Week 8–9
▶ Deliver coach/mentor training ▶ Promote the programme to the targeted learners	Week 10–11
▶ Induct learners ▶ Coach/mentor matching process	Week 12
▶ (Matching event) ▶ Event launch	Week 13
▶ Commence mentor/coach relationships	Week 14
▶ Support workshops (monthly)	On-going
▶ Collect mid-way feedback	On-going
▶ Conduct final evaluation	Completion

It is always best to leave a certain amount of leeway in setting target dates. For example, recruitment of coaches or mentors may be slow and you may have to resort to more active or rigorous methods in order to recruit them. It may mean that you need to alter your promotional materials to make the proposition more attractive, which all takes time. This will obviously impact on the training date, if previously set. You will probably not want to go ahead with the coach or mentor training if you only have three or four successful applicants. It may be that you are inundated with eager applicants and processing all the applications and interviewing takes more time than expected, especially if your applicants have time constraints on their availability for interview.

Before going ahead with any planned scheme, some thought should be given to your participants and whether your proposed timescales are likely to fit in with them. For example if you are offering academic support to undergraduates, then this should be offered at some stage during the beginning of the academic year but well before the exam period or course assignment deadlines. It may be that your programme is to be offered to those undertaking re-sits, but then you will need to consider whether your proposed coaches or mentors will be available at this time.

If planning a programme to support final-year students' transition into work or industry, then this is likely to be offered opportunely when they should be considering their career options. This however can be quite contentious, as was found with an alumni mentoring programme that was delivered in my own institution. Initially it was hoped to match second-year students to alumni who had been working for at least two years. This was to enable the undergraduates to consider work placements or the various career paths available to them in good time prior to completing their studies. However, in reality it was found that second-year students in most cases were not thinking this far ahead and consequently did not express an interest in this type of support. When the same opportunity was offered to final-year students the uptake was far greater. It is likely that the programme would have had even greater value had the students signed up to it a year previously, but it was better that they received some support, albeit later, rather than none at all. A compromise will need to be reached between the anticipated needs, what is known about your targeted group and their perceived needs. A case study for alumni mentoring can be found on page 134.

Another point to consider is the demands on your coaches and mentors. It may be that demand is high for academic support around exam time, but if you are using final-year students as your coaches or mentors, then they too will likely be less available to commit at this time. Being aware of not only your own and institutional diary commitments but those of your coaches, mentors, and learners is essential. Simple mistakes can then be avoided, such as booking a recruitment stand during 'reading week' when most students are not on campus. Particularly within a higher education context, a good knowledge of the academic diary for your institution is essential when planning.

▶ The Aims and Objectives

As has been seen in Chapter 3, there are a variety of reasons why it might be desirable to introduce a coaching or mentoring programme. Once you have established that there is a specific need within your institution to support a specific group of people, the next step is to consider whether that support is best offered by mentoring or coaching. For example, it may be found that International students have a lower retention rate than native students and it may be thought that this is due to language difficulties. If this is the case then perhaps offering 'language skills tutorials' delivered by a tutor may better help to resolve this issue than offering them a mentor or coach. However if it is found that lack of social integration is a key factor in the lower retention rate, then perhaps a mentor in their first few weeks may be the best solution. Despite the fact that I wholeheartedly support the process of mentoring and coaching, I accept that other support might better suit the purpose for some objectives. Seeking information from your target group can be extremely enlightening, as they will probably know best what has helped or will help them. It would be strongly advised to spend time conducting this research, collecting evidence of the need and possible solutions, before any time or funds are wasted on providing a coaching or mentoring programme that will not be utilised.

Once you have sufficient evidence to suggest that any coaching or mentoring offered will be taken up, then you will need to decide which will be the best group of people to provide the support. Whilst speaking to your targeted group, their opinions should be sought on this aspect too. It may be that they would prefer an experienced peer as a mentor to a member of staff. It may come to light that opinion is mixed on this, so a decision could then be taken to recruit mentors and coaches from perhaps members of staff and more experienced students so as to be able to provide both. Your final evaluation could determine not so much which of these mentor or coaching groups is more effective but perhaps what specific elements of the support are best provided by staff or by experienced peers.

There are usually alternative groups who can be utilised as mentors or coaches, and very often a combination of both or all of them can work very well. Take the example above whereby you are trying to address the lower retention rates of international students. What should be considered here is whether these first-year students would be best supported by 'home' students or students from their own country who are now in their final year. There are pros and cons to both of these approaches. A 'home' student, if well trained, will be able to provide support with familiarisation of university life as well as language/ communication but may not be able to empathise with the situation as well as a final-year international student who will have shared a similar experience. However, an international student, particularly if he or she shares the same native language, is perhaps more likely to converse in that language. Thus the mentees may not be encouraged to integrate with 'home' student peers and university life as well as if they were being supported by one of the 'home' students. Of course there are many solutions to these issues, such as encouraging mentors or coaches as far as possible to refrain from communicating in their native language or perhaps through careful matching. The best possible solution to this issue is to train your mentors and coaches to be aware of the issues and leave the learners to select the mentor or coach of their choice. Interestingly it has been found that some learners will specifically select someone from their home country usually if they are feeling homesick, whilst others specifically go for a 'home' student if they are particularly keen to improve their language skills. Adopting this method ensures that the learners utilise the support in the way that suits them best, although your coaches and mentors should have the potential issues mentioned above brought to their attention as part of the training process. This way they can avoid speaking all the time in their native language or be more aware of the increased issues around home-sickness when studying abroad. Culturally, this can be an enriching experience for both the learners and the coaches or mentors.

Using members of staff as mentors or coaches can also bring similar issues if implementing a coaching or mentoring programme for higher education students. Some students will not relate well to members of staff whilst others will. What has become very apparent in the evaluations that I have conducted is that peer-to-peer mentoring or coaching is highly valued. Being able to converse with someone who is of a similar age and has recently been through the same experiences is cited frequently as being the main reason for this. But having members of staff as mentors or coaches (as long as they are not involved in the teaching or assessment of their allocated learner) has advantages too. The main benefit is that members of staff have more longevity in the role than students who will inevitably complete their studies and move on. Members of staff also have the usual benefit of knowing the institution and processes better than students. In my own personal experience, when working with a student with financial difficulties, I was able to help support her in making an appointment with 'Student Finance' when she had been unable to do this for herself for many weeks. Just my being copied into an email (as a member of staff) was sufficient to secure an appointment for her which sadly would probably not have been the case if I had been a 'student' mentor. However I would certainly advocate against misusing this advantage for any member of university staff acting as a mentor or coach. Again a mixture of both staff and student mentors can work very well especially when allowing the learners to select from profiles.

5 Recruitment and Screening of Mentors and Coaches

Being unable to recruit a sufficient number of mentors or coaches is a frequent problem for many higher education institution coordinators but with the right approach and persistence this can be overcome. It is advisable to apply similar guidelines as you would if you were recruiting for a job role making few, if any, allowances. What needs to be avoided at all costs is accepting applicants who are not really suitable for the role in order to meet your target number. It is much wiser to stick firmly to your selection criteria and deliver a smaller programme. Alternatively, if there is time to extend your search to other groups or improve your promotional material or recruitment methods, then do so. Allowing less than suitable applicants to take part is likely to lead to the failure of the programme or at the very least to poor quality mentoring or coaching. It is tempting in some cases, and I have certainly personally made this mistake in the early days of my work. To give an example, I have interviewed very personable and able students who arrived slightly late to their interview without their giving any proper excuse. Against my better judgement I have given them the benefit of the doubt and offered them a place on the training, to which they also arrived late. If they have then subsequently gone on to be matched with a learner, inevitably they have been unpunctual for these meetings too, resulting, quite rightly, in complaints or poor feedback. Having fallen foul of this in the early days of delivery, I am now extremely rigid on the matter, and if a candidate has not met expectations at interview then she or he is not offered a place on the training. I would strongly advise readers to do the same.

Your recruitment process may sometimes result in borderline applicants who you are not one hundred per cent certain will make a good mentor or coach. It may be that they appeared a little self-absorbed at interview, demonstrated less than perfect listening skills, were too talkative or perhaps over- or under-confident. In these cases I would give the benefit of the doubt and offer them a place on the training. All candidates should be informed that being offered a place on the training does not automatically result in their becoming part of the programme and subsequently being matched with a learner. It may be that during the training it becomes apparent that one of your participants is unsuitable for the role or he or she does not pass the assessment process, which I would strongly advocate being incorporated.

Any borderline students can be observed during this time and eliminated, or they may well withdraw themselves from the programme which can be construed as a positive thing. Better that they withdraw at this time rather than after they are matched. A good rule of thumb is to invite three or four extra people to the training to counter this inevitable attrition.

Having trust in your judgement is essential, as is the aim to deliver an exemplary programme rather than a second-rate one. A smaller scheme than anticipated whose impact is nonetheless apparent and demonstrable is preferable by far to a larger programme that has had little, or even worse, no impact. As the programme is repeated, which it will be if successful, you will find that the numbers of volunteer mentors and coaches will increase organically through word of mouth. If there is 'bad press', this can hinder recruitment and so is best avoided at all costs. In my own experience many of the mentor and coach applicants recall having seen the opportunity advertised the previous year and were interested but did not actually apply at the time. When asked what prompted them to apply this particular year, they very often say that a friend became involved and recommended it. A good reputation is paramount to successful recruitment, and persistence will be rewarded. After 15 years of mentor and coach recruitment in one institution I now have the advantage of being quite discerning in coach and mentor selection and some years have been known to decline one in three applications. Those applicants who are declined are always offered feedback and invited to re-apply the following year, which many subsequently do.

If using staff or external mentors, then this selection process does become more difficult; however it is essential that they too undergo a selection procedure and are eliminated if deemed unsuitable. Some may feel that this selection process, when they are experienced working adults who are volunteering their time, is inappropriate. But, just because they are in employment does not automatically mean that they will be suitable for a mentoring or coaching role. If they willingly and successfully undergo the selection process, this in itself will be an indicator that they have an appreciation that the learners whom they will potentially be supporting have the right to be protected from being given inappropriate support. Those who object very strongly to undergoing the selection process will likely not be suitable for a mentoring or coaching role. Any feedback to rejected applicants in these cases will need to be extremely tactfully given, but in a number of cases it will be that time constraints in attending the training and support workshops will be the concern. Disappointing though it may be to lose applicants, if they are unable to commit to training and workshops, they would inevitably have discovered that finding time for meetings with their learner would have been prohibitive to their taking part too.

The following are examples of selection criteria guidelines, although these will differ according to the aims and objectives of your intended programme:

Undergraduate peer coaching with the aim of improving academic attainment

Essential

- Good communication and organisational skills
- Interpersonal skills
- Willingness to commit to training
- Willingness to commit to supporting another student for up to 15 weeks/ 1 hour per week
- Availability to attend fortnightly mentor support workshops
- An understanding of the importance of the need for commitment and consistency in meetings, emails, timing, etc.
- On track to receive at least a 2:1
- Not committed to more than 20 hours of paid work per week

Desired

- An understanding of the possible needs that others studying a similar course might face
- Experience of supporting others

Alumni mentoring with the aim of supporting final-year undergraduates into work

Essential

- Good communication and organisational skills
- Interpersonal skills
- Willingness to commit to training
- Endorsement from line manager to take part/commit
- Willingness to share experiences and knowledge
- Available for up to a 9-month period approximately 2 hours per fortnight
- An understanding of the importance of the need for commitment and consistency in mentoring meetings, emails etc.
- At least 1 year's experience in the workplace

Desired

- An understanding of the possible needs that students might face in their final year

▶ Experience of mentoring, coaching or supporting others
▶ A knowledge of job search activities, CV writing, interview techniques, etc.

Mentoring school pupils from lower socioeconomic backgrounds with the aim of motivating them to perform well academically and raise their aspirations towards higher education

Essential

▶ Good communication and organisational skills
▶ Interpersonal skills
▶ Willingness to commit to training
▶ Willingness to share experiences and knowledge
▶ Available for at least 1 hour per week during school time for a 15-week period
▶ Willingness to travel locally (expenses paid)
▶ An understanding of the importance of the need for commitment and consistency in mentoring meetings etc.
▶ A genuine interest in the development of young people
▶ A knowledge of the curriculum/education system
▶ Not committed to more than 20 hours of paid work per week

Desired

▶ An understanding of the possible barriers that pupils from low income families might face
▶ Experience of mentoring/supporting young people
▶ Access to own transport

Your interview questions and application form, between them, will allow applicants to demonstrate the required knowledge and understanding for your programme similarly to any other job application.

▶ **Mentor and Coach Promotion and Recruitment Methods**

A deep understanding and awareness of your targeted group will be essential, as any advertisement will need to be appealing to them. This will vary enormously from person to person. There is no one coach or mentoring promotional text that will be attractive to all, and the trick is to use appropriate terminology to highlight aspects of the programme that are likely to promote interest for them. For example if you are targeting psychology students to become coaches or mentors, then the following bullet points included in any advert are more likely to attract attention.

▶ Interested in helping others to overcome barriers and succeed?
▶ Do you want to develop your interpersonal and communication skills?
▶ Would you make a good role model?

The same wording would be less likely to appeal to students in usually more male-dominated subjects such as Engineering, Maths or Astronomy. It has been demonstrated that the bullet points below included in any advertising are more likely to attract mentors or coaches from these subject areas.

▶ Need experience to add to your CV?
▶ Want to develop your leadership skills?
▶ Improve your employability?

Slightly amending any advertisements depending on where and by whom they are going to be seen is very worthwhile. A 'one fits all' approach is unlikely to be successful and should be avoided.

Another factor in mentor and coach recruitment, if you are trying to attract higher education students, is their year of study. If you are hoping to recruit final-year students into your programme, then promoting it as an opportunity to increase their employability skills is likely to grab their attention. They will particularly be seeking opportunities to obtain some work experience at this stage. Those in their first year are more likely to be enticed by its being presented as a fun opportunity and a chance to meet other students.

Members of university staff and external business people will more likely be attracted to the opportunity to learn and develop coaching or mentoring skills. These are transferable skills that are commonly used in the workplace, and acquiring them may well improve their working relationships. Many people in these types of positions will be attracted to the altruistic nature of this type of programme alone but may have concerns about the time commitment.

It is also worth bearing in mind that future participant 'learners' may well read the promotional materials for your mentors and coaches, depending on where you place your advertisements. For this reason, although it is prudent to inform potential mentors of the benefits of the programme for the learners, not too much emphasis should be placed on this aspect at this stage. It is best to talk in more general terms of what you want to achieve by introducing the programme such as 'to help international students to make the best of the opportunities offered' or 'to improve the academic attainment of undergraduates in their first year'.

Be specific about your requirements such as being on track for a first class degree or two years' experience in the work place. It is also wise to be open about the commitment that you expect, which will include the training programme, attendance at support workshops, and of course the mentoring or coaching sessions. If you are offering any form of gratuity or payment it can also be mentioned, although rather than specify exactly what it will be, it can referred to as a 'token of appreciation' for the coaches'/mentors' commitment upon successful completion of the programme.

A powerful aid to mentor and coach recruitment for students is the endorsement of the scheme by programme tutors or other members of staff who actively promote it on your behalf. It has been noted on several occasions that where a member of staff emails their students informing them of the opportunity, applications received are particularly high. It is this dual approach by staff and the mentoring or coaching coordinator that is most successful.

The most effective approach of all to recruiting mentors and coaches is to arrange a short presentation or talk to the group of people whom you want to volunteer. Any presentation should be brief and start by informing them what mentoring and coaching are or are not. Let them know that it is not just telling someone what to do and when to do it and that it is a skilled approach that takes time to learn. Explain that they will receive thorough training and be supported throughout the process. You can also let them know what the commitment of their time is and what you hope to achieve from the programme. Quotes from previous participants, both learners and coaches or mentors, are also very influential especially if they validate any benefits for the coaches or mentors. It is important to point out that they too will reap benefits from taking part, such as improved leadership, team working and communication skills. Finally they should be informed how to apply. If possible leave time for questions but more importantly let them know that they can contact you for further information without being obliged to take part. As with any written advertisement the content of this talk should bear in mind your target audience and be amended accordingly. It can also be extremely convincing when one or two of your experienced mentors or coaches actually give the presentation themselves or contribute to it.

These ten-minute presentations can be given to students at the start of term at induction sessions or at the end or beginning of lectures or tutorials – as long as you have permission of course. This reiterates the need to engage and collaborate with other staff at your institution to allow these talks to take place. After 15 years of coaching and mentoring with programme tutors having seen the benefits for participating students, it is not uncommon for over 50 talks to be given during induction week, many of which have been requested by programme tutors. It is this type of activity that results in the numerous applications received each year.

Another tactic, apart from promoting the opportunity on posters and leaflets and the intranet, has been to directly target specific students. An example of this was when final-year Maths students were urgently required to support second-year students as there had been more applications for support than anticipated. It had not been possible to find an allocated slot within a lecture to deliver a presentation and so, having looked at their timetables, it was established where the target students would be at certain times of the day. Armed with leaflets, one or two coordinators approached students just as they were going into the lecture room or alternatively waited outside until they came out. Obviously many students were reluctant to stay and talk, but a reasonable number listened to the appeal given by the coordinators and were happy to take a leaflet away with them. Using this very direct approach was effective and was subsequently used for other subject areas in which there was a shortage of coaches.

An even more targeted approach is for programme tutors to personally approach suitable students and suggest that they apply. This can work particularly well for those who perhaps are lacking in confidence in their own abilities. An example of a typical successful advertisement for final-year or postgraduate students is shown in Figure 5.1:

Coaching & Mentoring Opportunities

▶ *Want to develop your leadership skills?*
▶ *Do you want to improve your interpersonal & communication skills?*
▶ *Would you like experience to add to your CV?*

Becoming a mentor or coach on one of our programmes could help you achieve all of these things and more. We are looking to recruit students in particular studying Sports Studies, Sports Science, and Dietetics to act as mentors (or coaches) in the academic year 2015/16. The commitment is likely to consist of weekly meetings with your allocated coachee/mentee for a 10–15 week period starting in November/December 2015.

You may be matched with a student who is new to the University to help them access the resources they need for their course and quickly adjust to university life. Or you might be matched with a student in their 2nd year who is having some difficulties with their course. The support given may be of a more academic nature, and some of the contact might be via email as well as face to face.

To be a part of the mentoring or coaching programmes you will need to attend the full 2-day training programme on

Wednesday 12th and Thursday 13th October 2015

A small bursary will be awarded to students who successfully complete the programme or a University Certificate will be awarded (upon successful submission of assessment criteria).

If you are interested in any of these schemes please email 'Administrator Name' and ask for an application form. For further details email findout-moreaboutmentoring@university.

Deadline for applications is 1st October 2015

Figure 5.1 Example of Mentor and Coach Recruitment Advertisement

For some programmes it may be that you are seeking mentors or coaches with particular knowledge or experience and this should be clearly stated in your advertisement. In some cases it may need to be worded very sensitively, such as when you would like to attract applicants from a specific ethnic or socioeconomic background. For some school mentoring programmes where you are anticipating supporting pupils who have been excluded from mainstream education, you may be interested to hear from applicants who have themselves been in a similar situation. A tactful approach to this is to state in the advertisement the aims and objectives of your programme, such as to support pupils who have been excluded from mainstream school or to support students who are the first in their family to enter higher education. You can then finish by saying that you would be particularly interested in hearing from applicants who have experienced and overcome such barriers.

Often it pays to place repeated advertisements but change the text and heading each time. Repeating the same advertisement can result in it being overlooked, but by changing the heading and content you are more likely to extend the appeal to a greater range of people. For example you might use the heading above, 'Mentoring & Coaching Opportunities', once or twice, then change it to 'Can you be a role model?' and later change it to 'Develop your leadership skills'. As has been previously discussed, it has been shown that some people only apply after seeing the advertisement two or even three times.

▶ Mentor and Coach Selection and Interview

Having set the dates for the training you will first need to select which of your applicants look suitable and then invite them for interview. It is wise to obtain as much information as possible about your applicants during the application process, and this information can be used later in the matching process.

An example application form can be seen in Appendix 2. You will see that it is quite a comprehensive form and not dissimilar to a job application. Whilst it may initially appear excessive for a voluntary mentoring or coaching role, by making completion of this a requirement you will ensure that only those who are truly committed will make the effort to apply. When working with undergraduates in particular, it is also extremely good practice for them in applying and preparing for job interviews. Completing the form should also help applicants to consider what they personally want to achieve from taking part and so prepare them for the interview stage.

Asking about their programme of study, grades, availability, different languages spoken, and access to transport may all prove very helpful later on in the matching process. If this information can all then be stored in a database, when you are later seeking a mentor or coach who speaks a specific language, then you will quickly be able to locate one with a find/search tool. Experience has shown that electronically storing as much information about your mentors and coaches as possible will save hours of time searching through application forms later on when you have a specific need for an applicant.

There may well be additional questions that you will need to add for your specific programme. This might be to ask them for details of optional modules that they are studying if it is an academic programme that you are implementing. Other possible optional questions could be to ask whether they are the first in their family to embark on a higher education course or perhaps whether they have a disability. The latter might be useful if you are proposing to support pupils or students with disabilities.

It is always wise to include equal opportunities monitoring information too which should of course not be used for the selection process. The format of these monitoring questions should be readily available at your own institution. It should be quite apparent when reading the completed application forms which of your applicants appear to be suitable, and then you should invite them in for a short interview.

Interviews

The interview does not necessarily need to be lengthy and even 10–15 minutes may be sufficient. As you already have quite comprehensive information on the application form, the interview just serves the purpose of checking that the information given is accurate and allows the candidates the opportunity to elaborate. It is the willingness to attend the interview that is important and an opportunity to check their punctuality.

For those who are experienced in conducting job interviews, the same rigour should be applied despite it being for a much shorter duration. It is recommend that two people conduct the interview if possible in order that each can make notes and discuss the merits or otherwise of each applicant. This can be particularly important in the case of being uncertain of a candidate's suitability.

An 'equal opportunities' approach should be used, the same questions being asked of each applicant with a scoring system devised to record the quality of their answers. Another advantage of having two interviewers is that one coordinator can ask the applicant the questions whilst the other can make notes on the answers given. This avoids leaving the applicant looking at the tops of the interviewer's heads which can be unnerving, particularly for an undergraduate who may have little interview experience. It also allows the person asking the questions to maintain eye contact which can help to make the interviewee feel more at ease.

As in any interview situation you would want to put your applicants at ease, and it is always good practice to offer them the opportunity of asking questions at the end which of course should be answered as truthfully as possible. Often these questions can reveal more about your applicant. For example by asking a question that was answered in your promotional material (e.g. about the target group or the aims of the programme) they reveal that they have not thoroughly prepared for the interview. Some may just ask for clarification of how much and when they will be paid. This could be an indication that their motive for taking part is purely financial which may not be ideal. It would be hoped that any question asked would be an insightful one about the targeted learners or perhaps a practical or logistical one (e.g. where do the coaching/mentoring sessions take place).

Some interview questions suggested in Table 5.1 below will be a good starting point for any mentoring or coaching programme. It would not be recommended to ask any more than six set questions, as the ones below will inevitably lead to more conversation and further questions or clarification anyway. You may find that these questions will confirm quite quickly that your applicant is indeed suitable for the role or is unsuitable, although some may leave you in doubt. As has been previously suggested, any for whom you do still have some doubt may be invited to the training which will allow for further observation.

Table 5.1 Suggested Interview Questions

Questions	Notes	Score 1 = Poor 5 = Excellent
Please tell us why you are interested in taking part in this programme.	This question will give you an insight into what promoted their interest which might vary from wanting to help others to enhancing their CV. It will often result in their divulging personal experiences that are relevant to your programme aims and objectives.	
Please tell us about any previous experience you have of mentoring/coaching or supporting others.	This can lead to the applicant elaborating on past experiences which in turn will allow you to determine whether they have a genuinely caring nature and willingness to help others.	
Please tell us what you understand mentoring or coaching to be.	Although they do not have to have a precise answer this question can often reveal any applicants whose main objective is to tell and advise others what they should be doing. It can also reveal where an applicant has taken the trouble to research more information on the subject.	
What qualities do you have that you believe would make you a successful mentor or coach?	A revealing question that can establish how much understanding they have of the role as well as their suitability for it.	
What kind of support do you think first-year higher education students/school pupils might need?	This question will reveal how much empathy the applicant might have with your targeted group of learners. It can often reveal applicants who have a narrow outlook and only have the ability to view things from their own perspective	
What difficulties might a mentor or coach encounter in the role?	This question can often reveal a lack of confidence in the applicant in their own abilities. It may also reveal a greater or lesser understanding of the role.	
Communication skills	There is no need to ask a specific question about communication skills, but the interviewer/s should assess the applicant's listening and speaking skills.	
Comments	Here you might ask specific questions that are pertinent to your specific programme, such as what location suits them best, whether they will remain at university and be available during Christmas or summer breaks, or have their own transport, etc.	

In some cases, particularly when applicants talk about their reasons for applying for the role, the interview can lead to them revealing very personal information. Many applicants talk about being inspired by a mentor when they were young and the experience turning their life around. They talk about being put on the right path or being supported by someone at a troubled time in their lives which has made them want to 'give something back'. It is not uncommon for applicants to become very emotional when recalling and talking about these experiences. However caution is advised should your interviewee become very upset. It may be that there are still some underlying issues that could be exacerbated by supporting someone else who is very troubled. In some cases these feelings could be problematic if they are shared and discussed within the coaching or mentoring sessions, thereby taking the focus away from the learner. It may be wise to have an open discussion with the applicant if this is the case, expressing your concerns about their welfare. In some cases it may be decided not to employ them this year but to allow them to fully resolve their own issues before embarking on your programme, perhaps the following year. It may also be prudent to signpost them to other sources of support available. Being aware that they are vulnerable can also help in the matching process, should you decide to employ them. In one instance a recovering, but not yet fully recovered, anorexic mentor was matched with another young person who had an eating disorder. This culminated in a very rewarding and beneficial relationship for both the mentor and the learner. However it was very closely monitored by the coordinator who ensured that the mentoring did not adversely affect the mentor.

The scores of each interviewer should be added up or alternatively they can be agreed for each applicant between you. It is best to allow five minutes after each interview to do this to avoid confusion, especially if you are interviewing several candidates. It is wise to set a 'pass' mark prior to interview and for the suggested questions above a maximum of 35 points is available. Your pass mark can be adjusted according to the calibre and number of your applicants. If you have 25 available places on the training and 50 applicants, your pass mark is likely to be high and in the region of 28 out of 35. I would certainly not advocate lowering it below 21 for the questions in the example, even if you have very few applicants. It would be more prudent to re-advertise the position. It would also be preferable not to have any one question score lower than two.

Taking notes and scoring applicants in this way will allow you to give comprehensive feedback to any applicants who are turned down. This of course should be carried out very sensitively and in a way that allows the applicant to learn from the experience. There have been many applicants in my experience who initially applied for a mentoring or coaching role but did not sufficiently prepare for interview, who then went on to successfully apply the following year.

Following this procedure makes the process transparent and defensible and ultimately will result in your recruiting high-calibre mentors and coaches. This will in turn give your programme the greatest possible chance of success.

▶ Police Screening of Applicants

If your mentors or coaches are to be working with children or vulnerable people, then it will be essential that some form of police check is carried out prior to their being matched. The procedure for this will vary from country to country, but most checks are likely to incur a cost of some kind which will need to be accounted for in your costings.

This clearance procedure can take some time, and so it is advisable that the process is started as early as possible so as not to delay the matching process. An opportune time would be as soon as an applicant is accepted onto the programme and invited to the training. In the event of the applicant not being given clearance, then a fair process will need to be put into place to determine whether he or she can be deemed suitable for a mentoring or coaching role or not. It may be that he or she committed a minor offence as a young teenager and received no further convictions since. You may consider that this should not prevent him or her from taking part in your programme; however a robust process is essential in order to make this decision. A proper risk assessment is vital to ensure the protection and safety of your intended learners.

A process should be established for a panel to make a judgement on whether any offence committed is major enough to prevent a candidate from being a mentor or coach on your programme. Your potential mentor or coach should have the opportunity to discuss the offence with the panel and offer her or his explanation of the event and circumstances. After these discussions, a decision should be made collectively by the panel as to whether the potential coach or mentor poses any risk to your learners. If notes are kept of this meeting and the decision made to allow her or him to take part, then there will be written evidence that you took the necessary precautions to protect your participants. If however the panel decides not to allow the applicant to take part, then clear reasons as to why this decision was made should be provided for her or him. Whilst you may wish to give people a 'second chance', protection of your learners is paramount. In one case, an undergraduate who had a conviction five years previously for possession of class B drugs was permitted to work as a peer coach to fellow students but not allowed to work with pupils in a school. Another student was not allowed to participate in the mentoring programme at all as there had been two convictions for 'drink driving' and one for driving without insurance, the most recent being within the last year. It was agreed by the panel that because of the multiple offences, this student was more likely to reoffend and would not be a particularly suitable role model for younger students. Each case needs to be considered individually, and following a procedure such as the one above provides a balance between potential risks and offering applicants a fair opportunity.

6 Mentor and Coach Training

Probably one of the most important aspects of implementing a mentoring or coaching programme is the training programme offered to the mentors and coaches. Too many coordinators assume that if they have followed rigorous selection procedures, they will have high-calibre mentors or coaches who will need little training. However the training is essential in order to thoroughly convey the programme objectives and emphasise their commitment. They should then be taught the underpinning knowledge and skills behind successful mentoring or coaching although many of your group may feel that they have already acquired these skills. Due to the many misconceptions about the interventions, it is imperative that they are led through the process and taught the skills as you wish them to be practised.

To fully cover every aspect of the coaching or mentoring process will require at least two days of training. Day one will cover the remit of the programme and some of the basic requirements such as confidentiality and when/if to disclose information, plus the skills required such as active listening, questioning, and action planning. Day two should be an opportunity to apply some of the skills to common scenarios and to introduce some of the mentoring or coaching tools. The sample training programme found in Appendix 3 provides suggested activities and exercises that enable the participants to learn the skills without the need for endless Powerpoint slides or role play (the latter very often being one of the most dreaded aspects of this type of training).

The training programme is also invaluable in that it allows you to observe your participants, detecting any weaknesses or strengths, identifying any that are unsuitable. This will not only help in the matching process but is also an opportunity for you to build rapport with them, making it easier to support them throughout the programme. It is essential that a relationship of mutual trust is built between you. You need to be confident that they have the required skills to support your learners and they need to feel confident that they will be supported during the process and not put into any awkward or uncomfortable situations.

The training programme should be thought of as an extension to the interview process. Your participants should have been informed that an invitation to the training did not guarantee them a place on the programme. Acceptance will be subject to them demonstrating the skills during the course of the training and also on passing a short assessment at the end.

For example a student who is late arriving for the training on both training days should not be included in the programme unless there are exceptional mitigating circumstances. Similarly students who continually monopolise the group discussions during the training sessions with anecdotes about their own experiences are likely to do this in their mentoring or coaching sessions and therefore not practice good mentoring or coaching skills. Using a 'red-flag' system like the one below in Table 6.1 will enable you to record any concerns during the training. It will be particularly useful in the event of having different trainers on day one and day two. A good rule to follow is to not employ anyone on your scheme who has accumulated two or more 'red flags' over the two days.

Table 6.1 Training Observation Record

Instructions: Mark in the appropriate box when a participant has shown evidence that he or she might lack the required quality/skill needed for the role. Note the actual evidence for this in the last column.

Name	Late	Op	Li	In	PMC	UP	Evidence

Key:

Late = arriving late to sessions

Op = opinionated/unwilling to consider others' opinions

Li = poor listening skills

In = poor interpersonal skills

PMC = poor mentoring/coaching skills

UP = unwillingness to participate

To enable close observation of your participants, no more than 20–25 participants should be trained at one time and then it would be best to have two trainers. One experienced trainer should be able to both train and observe up to 12–15 participants with relative ease. As part of the training there will be group work exercises, and having a good ratio of trainers to participants will allow for each group to be observed in turn and for a trainer to lead or direct discussions whilst they are working.

Basic Mentor or Coach training should comprise at the very least the following components:

▶ Introduction to the mentoring or coaching programme and the expected commitment
▶ Addressing any concerns that the participants have about taking part in the programme
▶ Establishing boundaries for the mentoring or coaching relationship/contracting
▶ What are mentoring/coaching and how do they differ from other supportive relationships?
▶ The skills required for a successful mentor/coach
▶ Confidentiality or disclosure using case studies
▶ Listening skills – developing a good listener into an active listener
▶ Effective questioning
▶ Preparing for the first session
▶ Action planning, target setting, and giving appropriate feedback
▶ Record-keeping requirements
▶ Common issues and how to deal with them
▶ Introduction to the mentoring/coaching toolkit and resources
▶ Applying tools to some of the more common issues
▶ Practice coaching and mentoring sessions
▶ Assessment scenario
▶ Plenary to include a re-visit of the concerns raised on Day 1 and practical issues/reminder of the requirements for the specific programme
▶ Evaluation feedback on the training programme

The sample training plan can be found in Appendix 3, although the content will vary to some degree depending on the aims and objectives of your programme. If, for example, you are training mentors to support students in seeking employment and career opportunities, you may wish to devote some of the training to introducing them to the resources that will be available to them. If the programme will utilise ementoring, then a session will need to be included to highlight the differences between this form of communication and face-to-face sessions. The order of the training sessions too can be adjusted, although it is best to adhere to a logical progression.

A suggested format and suggested activities for the sessions can be as follows:

1. Introductory Session
This will reiterate the aims and objectives for your programme and what commitment is expected from your participants. It is wise to explain at this

stage that the training programme will form part of the assessment and that there will be a short assessment at the end to check their understanding of the process. An agenda should also be distributed for the two days of training, so that participants know what to expect.

It should be emphasised that no allowances will be made for people who request to leave for part of the training due to prior commitments etc. Attendance for the whole duration is necessary and is also a sign of their commitment. If the training days have been set and known for several weeks then there are no real excuses as to why any of your participants should not be able to attend. You will quickly find that if you make allowances for one person then others will soon follow suit, and so it is best to maintain a firm approach. For any that do have mitigating circumstances that prevent their attendance for either part or all of the training, then perhaps alternative training days can be offered (assuming that you have a sufficient number of applicants).

2. Icebreaker
As with most training sessions it is always good to have an icebreaker session to relax people and let them start to get to know each other. By asking them to work in pairs to find out specific information about each other without writing it down, you will already be testing their listening skills. Examples might be to find out what their partners are studying, why they applied to be a mentor/coach, and the most useful thing that they have learned whilst studying at university or when starting work. Introducing their partner with the information that they have found out rather than just introducing themselves will also be a test of their interpretive and listening skills. Even at this early stage you may identify participants who have not demonstrated good listening either by misunderstanding information that was told to them or in some cases by them stating that they ran out of time when it came to their turn to ask the questions! It may be that you have other trusted icebreakers that you use successfully, which is perfectly acceptable.

3. Concerns
Although this can set a slightly negative tone for the start of the training, it is a good method of revealing any worries that your participants may have. There should be only one concern written on each post-it note so that they can be grouped into themes, although they can write down as many concerns as they wish. Knowing what these concerns are can also ensure that you will be able to allay some of these fears during the course of the training. Whilst the majority of the concerns are likely to be around having sufficient time to take part or not being of any use to their learner (demonstrating a lack of confidence), they may also reveal some misconceptions about the expectations. You may often find concerns such as a fear of giving the incorrect advice to

their learner. Hopefully by the end of the training your participants will be fully conversant with the idea that there will be little need to give advice if they follow the correct procedure for asking good open questions, exploring options, and action planning. The aim of this exercise is not to answer all these concerns immediately but to bring them out into the open so that they can be referred to and addressed during the course of training.

If the post-its are stuck onto the wall, participants should be invited to add to them should anything else come to mind. Once the training programme has finished they should be revisited to check that all the concerns have been responded to over the course of the training, and if not, the remaining concerns should be discussed at this time.

This of course does not mean that your participants should not feel free to ask questions at any stage during the training.

4. Ground Rules/Setting the Boundaries

This part of the session is to establish that mentoring/coaching requires an agreement between two people and for it to work well an agreement should be made between them as to how it will work best. The first session should not be a time for the mentor or coach to tell the learner what they expect if they are to support them.

Ask the participants what they would like to see happen during the training to ensure that they learn, that all the material is covered, and that it is an enjoyable and informative experience for all. Hopefully they will suggest things such as listening to and respecting each others' opinions, everyone participating, not ridiculing anyone who asks a question, keeping mobile phones switched off or on silent, not monopolising the discussions, and being punctual. If everyone is agreed that something would be a good 'ground rule', then write it on your Powerpoint list. If need be, participants should be prompted to talk about confidentiality. Should they impart personal information about themselves during the training, it would hopefully be agreed that anything personal discussed within the group is not disclosed to anybody else, including friends, family, etc.

Once you have exhausted your list then you ask whether these things are appropriate within your mentoring or coaching relationship. Everything that has been written down should usually be included, with the exception of 'confidentiality'. It is at this point that you ensure that your participants are aware that, whilst the nature and content of their discussions with their learner should indeed be confidential, this would be with one exception. The exception would be if their learner disclosed something that led them to believe that he or she was in danger of being harmed, causing harm to others, or involved in criminal activity. Participants should be reassured that this will be covered as part of the training and that the coordinator will be available to support them should this occur.

An agreement such as the one in Table 6.2 can be utilised for the purpose of noting and discussing the terms of the agreement.

Table 6.2 Example of a Coach/Mentor and Learner Agreement

MENTORING/COACHING AGREEMENT

We are both voluntarily entering into this partnership which can be terminated by either of us at any time. However in the event of any misunderstanding or disagreement we will endeavour to resolve these before deciding to terminate the agreement.

We agree that...

1. The mentoring/coaching relationship will last for approximately _____ weeks/ months. This period will be reviewed monthly and will end by amicable agreement once we have achieved as much as possible.

2. We will meet at least once every _____ (week/fortnight/month). Meeting times, once agreed, should not be cancelled unless this is unavoidable and where possible at least _____ hours'/days' notice will be given. At the end of each meeting we will agree a date for the next meeting.

3. Each meeting will last a minimum of _____ minutes and a maximum of _____ minutes.

4. The aim of the mentoring/coaching is to discuss and help the learner to achieve the following goals but these can be reviewed and changed accordingly:

    a)
    b)
    c)

5. We agree that the role of the mentor/coach is to:

    _____
    _____
    _____

6. We agree that the role of the learner is to:

    _____
    _____
    _____

7. We agree to keep the general content of these meetings confidential except in exceptional circumstances such as when there is a worry about the person's safety or well-being.

Mentor signature .... Mentee signature ....

Date ....

---

5. What Are Mentoring and Coaching?

This section of the training should be extremely thorough as you will be establishing the skills that are required for the role. You will need sets of cards such as the ones shown in Table 6.3 with the following mentor or coach attributes, although these can be changed to suit your particular programme.

Table 6.3 Mentor or Coach Skills and Attributes for training purposes

Sense of Humour	Questioning	Listening	Exploring Options	Empathy
Proactive	Action Planning	Able to give feedback	Honesty	Time Management
Patience	Sympathy	Problem Solving	Subject Expert	Advising
Consistency	Enthusiasm	Challenging	Knowledge of University	Counselling

In small groups of 3–5 people, your participants should sort the cards in order from the least important attributes for a mentor or coach to the most important (with 'important' and 'not so important' in the middle). This should be completed after comprehensive discussions within their groups (ensuring that the 'ground rules' previously established are adhered to). There should be no more than five skills cards under each of the four headings.

Once all the groups have agreed on the order importance for the skills for a mentoring role, then they should walk around to see what the other groups have decided, noting where there are extreme differences of opinion. Once this is completed each group should return to their set of cards so that they can justify their decisions in the ensuing discussions. Each of the cards should be discussed with the whole group, and it will be revealed that all of the skills/attributes are likely to be important at some stage in the mentoring or coaching relationship apart from a couple of 'red herrings'. The latter are 'advising' and 'counselling' which are to be avoided. It should be pointed out that whilst a mentor or coach will adopt some similar approaches to that of a counsellor such as listening and questioning, the support will not be therapeutic and they can refer their learner to a counselling service should it become necessary. They should also be reminded that becoming a counsellor takes several years of training and they will only have two days in which to complete their training.

Similarly, 'advising' should be referred to as an approach that should only be used infrequently if at all. They should be encouraged to mainly ask questions, explore options, action plan and give feedback to their learner which is likely to achieve greater long-term success and self-efficacy. If using these attributes there should be little necessity for 'problem solving'. Being a 'subject expert' or having 'knowledge of University' are not particularly vital, as mentors and coaches should be able to source any information that they don't know on behalf of their learner if necessary.

The cards can be adjusted to suit your specific needs although the suggested ones in Table 6.3 are particularly pertinent to a peer mentoring or coaching relationship. It should be established that some of the attributes are only appropriate at particular stages in the relationship. For example it would not be wise to 'challenge' a learner's behaviour if you are in the early stages of the relationship and have not yet built sufficient rapport. However, challenging learners who constantly arrive late to your meetings or blame other people for their failings will be a necessary part of the role.

Another point that will need to be made if training for an academic mentoring or coaching programme is for the coaches and mentors to have an awareness and understanding of the danger of plagiarism and collusion. Your mentors or coaches need to ensure that they do not share their previous academic work with their learners. In addition they will need to be made aware of the dangers of actually doing work for their learners, which is of course unacceptable. The boundaries of the relationship will need to be clearly set out within the training and accompanying resources.

6. Building a Relationship

This exercise is useful in establishing the nuances between different relationships. When split into small groups and given a particular relationship (e.g. Line Manger/Employee or Parent/Child or Friends) the group should list all the elements that make it a good one. They are likely to come up with several aspects such as trust, respect, affection and understanding. Each group can talk through their allocated relationship and why each element is important. As a whole group you can then explore which of these elements is important or inappropriate for mentor- or coach-learner relationship. This will help the participants to recognise the differences between these relationships, establish where a mentoring or coaching sits, and explore the boundaries between them.

An alternative to this session to establish the nature of a mentoring or coaching role could be a tick list of mentor statements such as the following:

▶ A mentor should regularly check that the mentee has achieved her or his targets/grades
▶ A mentor should be a role model/someone the mentee can aspire to be

▶ A mentor should demonstrate how to perform better in areas where the mentee is underperforming

▶ A mentor should provide support for the mentee with the issues of his or her choice

▶ A mentor should advise on how to improve a mentee's performance

▶ A mentor should organise and plan the mentee's time

▶ A mentor should have informal but regular meetings with her or his mentee in order to build up a 'friendship'

▶ A mentor should ensure that the mentee remains within the school/ college/ university

▶ A mentor should talk openly about his or her own experiences so that the mentee can learn from them

▶ A mentor should challenge the mentee when their opinions differ

▶ A mentor should keep the mentee's tutor/line manager updated on her or his progress

These can be passed around or stuck onto the wall. Each participant can tick or cross each statement, indicating agreement or disagreement. The trainer can then discuss each of the answers, as they are likely to contain a mixture of crosses and ticks, noting the differences of opinions. The statements are deliberately contentious and designed to promote discussion. Some of the statements are quite inappropriate, such as a mentor keeping a tutor/line manager updated on progress. To regularly report back to a tutor on progress is a breach of the confidentiality of the mentoring relationship. Often participants will feel that it is inappropriate to challenge a mentee whose opinion differs from his or her own. However, challenging (in a nonaggressive way) is often part of a mentoring or coaching role, particularly when a learner continually blames others for her or his own failure. These discussions can serve as a powerful lesson about the nature and complexity of a mentoring or coaching role.

7. Assumptions
This is a quick exercise that often highlights how humans have a tendency to make assumptions or pre-judge people even if it is done subconsciously or without malice. Ask the group to call out any assumptions that they have made about you in the short space of time that they have known you. Their suggestions might be based on some observation such as seeing that you have an athletic build and assuming that you play sport or exercise frequently. Encourage them to come up with as many things as possible without confirming or denying them. It is likely that as many of their suggestions, which will vary from what car you drive to what your hobbies are, will

be accurate as inaccurate. There is no particular need to reveal the correct answers, but you can give examples of where they were very inaccurate. Once it is established that incorrect assumptions can easily be made they can then be reminded that within a mentoring and coaching context it is essential not to make any judgements about your learners and that they should be allowed to tell you about themselves in their own time. From the way a person dresses or simply from his or her posture we will often assume things that may or may not be true. Many people who are feeling vulnerable or lacking in confidence will overcome this by conveying a tough exterior, sometimes appearing to others quite belligerent.

8. Communication

Sitting back to back with a partner, participants are asked to describe a simple picture to their partner. However, they are only allowed to use simple directions and geometric shapes rather than nouns to describe the picture (such as draw a straight line from the top of the page to the bottom or draw a circle, 2cm in diameter in the centre of the page). Their partner is not allowed to ask questions but simply draw what they have been instructed to do so. The describer is not permitted to look at what their partner is drawing until they have finished describing. This is usually a good demonstration of how much we rely on those nonverbal aspects of communication that we all take for granted. Some of the drawings are likely to be quite accurate and this can often be attributed to it being a universally familiar drawing of a cat or house, for example, rather than it being described very accurately. In the ensuing discussions it can be highlighted that where what it is being described becomes apparent quite quickly for the person who is drawing, the whole process is much simpler. The description does not need to be so detailed once the drawer knows what it is they are supposed to be drawing. This becomes a shared understanding which can be likened on occasion to a mentoring or coaching relationship.

9. Listening Skills

Ask the participants to work in pairs (A and B) with group A leaving the room. Group A is simply instructed to think of a favourite holiday or similar topic to tell their partner about upon their return. Group B (out of earshot of group A) is asked to firstly listen very intently to their partner when they come back into the room. At an agreed signal by the trainer (a cough or sitting down in a chair) they should stop listening or showing interest without being too obvious. They should stop asking questions, reduce eye contact, look out of a window or at their watch, etc. This is a good demonstration of the difference between good and poor listening. It will become very apparent when you give the signal to 'stop listening' as the conversation will lessen very rapidly. As soon as the person who is talking becomes aware that they are not being listened to, they will automatically stop talking. It quickly demonstrates the importance of always giving the learner your full attention.

10. Listening Skills Questionnaire

To complete this section of the training it can be very useful for your participants to complete a listening skills questionnaire. This can highlight the different aspects of listening and enable them to identify when they find it more difficult to focus such as when someone speaks very slowly or monotonously or with a strong accent. Discussions on how to overcome their identified areas for development should be held. An example of a listening skills questionnaire can be found in Appendix 4, and there are numerous versions freely available on the web.

11. Body Language

The previous exercises will lead to discussions about what signifies that we are listening to somebody else. Things such as nodding, tilting the head to one side, and learning forwards can all be indicators of good listening. It can be useful to show Powerpoint slides or videos of people interacting in order that the participants can comment on whether they are being attentive or not. These discussions should highlight actions that demonstrate that you are not actively listening, from too little eye contact to glancing at your watch, and any gender differences that may impact on a mentoring or coaching relationship. It should bring an awareness of not only the participants' own body language but that of their potential learners.

Asking two volunteers to arrange furniture as they would for a mentoring or coaching session can also be very revealing, especially when the rest of the group are invited to comment on the arrangement. Some will arrange the chairs with a table between them, whilst others will leave the table out altogether and put the chairs side by side but slightly facing each other. The exercise also demonstrates that whilst some of us will view the table as a barrier that might impede communication or perhaps as a sign of superiority, others will find it useful particularly when there are documents that both the learner and mentor or coach may want to look at.

The needs of the learner do need to be taken into account when thinking of the seating arrangements and it is a good opportunity at this point to highlight the fact that the meeting place is very important. Where one learner may feel quite relaxed at one venue, it might be quite unsuitable for others. An extreme example of this was seen when the learner had ADHD (Attention Deficit Hyperactivity Disorder) and was uncomfortable sitting and talking for long periods of time. After some discussions it was agreed that they would conduct their sessions whilst walking to a coffee shop approximately 20 minutes away and after having a coffee would then walk back to the campus. This became the format for their sessions and suited them very well.

Meeting at the private residence of either the mentor/coach or learner is inadvisable and so too is the coach's or mentor's place of work, unless it is specifically for a career mentoring programme and part of the intended session. Meeting at a coach's, mentor's, or learner's place of work can lead to distractions or disturbances, and so a mutually convenient venue such as a bookable meeting room or coffee bar (as long as it is not too busy) should be arranged. In working with children or young people there are many more restrictions to the meeting venue, which will be covered in Chapter 12.

12. Speaker/Listener/Observer

This exercise is simply a practice session allowing each participant to have a conversation on a specified topic or to observe, taking into account all the previous discussions. In triads each member of the group will have the opportunity to observe the others having their conversation taking note of the actions or questions that promote good conversation or perhaps impede it. It is also an opportunity for them to give each other feedback.

13. Questioning

There are a number of ways to put the message across about the importance of asking 'good' questions in coaching and mentoring, and depending on the current knowledge of your participants you may need to go through all three suggested activities until they have developed a deeper understanding.

A useful start can be to put some sample questions up on a Powerpoint slide and ask them what 'type of question' these are as well as whether they would be a good type of question to use in a mentoring or coaching context. Closed/open question examples should be used, moving on to examples of reflective questions such as 'What else might you have done in that situation?' and hypothetical questions such as 'So what do you think your tutor would say if you did that?' You should also cover probing questions, giving an example such as 'You say that you don't get on well with him, why do you think this is?' and also clarifying questions or statements such as 'So am I right in thinking that...?' You should also include examples of rhetorical and leading questions such as 'I'm sure that you can see the benefit of this, can't you?'

It is worth including in the discussions 'multiple questions' where too many questions are asked within the same sentence, likely leading to them remaining unanswered or confusing the learner. It should be pointed out that asking rhetorical and leading questions is extremely poor practice and serves only to impose the coach's or mentor's views onto the learner.

Having reminded the participants of the different question types, it can be useful for them each to be given a hand-out containing examples of poor questions. Individually or in small groups they should be given some time to re-phrase them. For example they can be given the closed question 'Are you enjoying your course?' Hopefully they will be able to devise more productive ones such as 'What aspects of your course do you enjoy most?' These can be discussed as a group in order that participants can learn from one another's examples.

The third suggested session would be to place participants in pairs with each taking a turn to be deliberately obstructive and uncommunicative whilst their partner attempts to find out more information about a given topic. This will force them to practise asking good questions and avoid using closed ones.

14. Value Judgements
This can be a good activity, particularly in the late afternoon if the group appear to be flagging in energy. Name three 'stations' around the room 'yes', 'no', and 'don't know' and ask the suggested questions in the training plan in Appendix 3 that are deliberately quite contentious, requesting them to be very honest with their answers. Once they are standing at the 'station' of their choice, you can then ask some individuals why they are there and what are their reasons. For example when asking if they would ride a motorbike and some people are standing by 'No', they might answer that they wouldn't as it is dangerous and a friend of theirs was badly injured whilst riding one. Someone from the 'Yes' group might respond by saying that it is cheaper to run than a car and exhilarating to ride. It should not be allowed to progress into a debate or argument about what is right or wrong. Having worked through the questions and hearing the different reasons for people making their choices it is valuable to point out that everyone's views are quite valid and they have mostly come to those views because of their past experiences. In coaching and mentoring it is not appropriate to make any judgements about the learners' views and opinions but more important to find out why they have those values or opinions. It is certainly not the remit of a coach or mentor to change their learners' views to match their own or bring them round to their way of thinking.

15. Disclosure
The best way to convey the importance of this topic is to distribute case studies to small groups for discussion, and these should be reasonably realistic within the context of your mentoring or coaching programme. An example

may be of a young girl studying at the university who is very thin, lethargic and pale and who tells the mentor in their third session that she is on a strict diet and sometimes induces vomiting. Questions to set to each group should be 'What would they do/say?' and 'What action, if any, would they take?' Other examples could be a scenario in which one of the learners has admitted in the coaching or mentoring session to taking drugs on occasion or someone has disclosed feeling suicidal following the exam results or perhaps has admitted to self-harming.

Each group can decide their best course of action and whether the information should be disclosed immediately to someone else. Discussions need to take place about the possible consequences of doing so such as a betrayal their learner's trust which may result in a breakdown of the relationship. Not disclosing, on the other hand, may result in harm coming to the learner. Participants should be reassured that in cases such as these the coordinator should be consulted and so a decision can be made about the best course of action to follow. In the event of being extremely concerned about the welfare of their learner, emergency services or the medical centre can be contacted. Participants should also be reassured at this stage that these types of occurrences in a coaching or mentoring relationship are extremely rare, although it would be negligent not to prepare for such eventualities. In my 15 years of supervising thousands of mentors and coach relationships, just one serious issue requiring disclosure has occurred. However it has been necessary on a handful of occasions to guide a mentor or coach through a period of concern for her or his learner which is the responsibility of the coordinator.

In the event that your participants will be working with children or young people, the guidelines will be more stringent and there will be set procedures in place within the school or other institution that they are attending.

16. Common Issues

This is a good exercise to both highlight the common issues that your mentors and coaches might encounter during their relationships and to help them prepare. Approximately six different 'issues' should be written down with blank flip chart paper beside them. Each participant should read the issue and write down one question that they would ask in that scenario or an action that they would take. If they already agree with what someone else has written, then they can mark it with a tick it to indicate this. Examples of some common issues could be as follows:

Example 1
Richard was late for the first meeting, saying that he went to the wrong room, and failed to turn up at all for the second session, saying that he

forgot. He was over 20 minutes late for the third session, saying that he was delayed, and you consequently lost half of the session.

Example 2
Daryl has turned up on time for the last three meetings but is very uncommunicative. He says that he doesn't really know what he wants to work on.

Example 3
David is enjoying his course apart from when he has to give oral presentations. His group are all well prepared, but the thought of presenting his part is making him feel unwell. He is thinking of asking his tutor to be excused or going off sick on the day.

Example 4
You are supporting Jenny who is soon to complete her Psychology Course. She says that she wants to continue on to a postgraduate master's degree in Occupational Psychology but has no work experience and has had to re-sit many of her modules. She is in danger of failing her final year completely if her grades continue to be so poor.

Example 5
Charlotte is very shy and in her first year at the university. She says that she doesn't get on with any of the people in her class and hasn't made any friends. She says that she doesn't have shared interests with any of them.

Example 6
Caroline has sent you a copy of her CV as she has a job to apply for by the end of the next day. This is the first time that you have been asked to look at the CV although you have been supporting Caroline for two months. It is a very poor CV that needs extensive amendments, but you have several work commitments that leave you very little spare time at least for the next three days.

These common issues can be amended to be specific to your particular programme and anticipated issues. Once everyone has contributed to each scenario, then a group discussion should be held debating the merits of each question or action.

17. Goal Setting
A Powerpoint presentation can be used to demonstrate Kolb's experiential learning cycle which describes the mentoring or coaching process quite well. It is the process of reflection, analysis, and planning in which the

mentor or coach can support their learner who will then have the 'concrete experience' on their own. This cycle is likely to be repeated several times over the course of their relationship with different actions being explored and/or agreed.

It is also a good opportunity to discuss the usual four cycles or stages of a mentoring or coaching relationship. Stage 1 will be when they are building rapport and this could take anything from one session to six or seven. With some learners it will be relatively easy to build rapport if they have much in common, but for others it may take longer to build up a mutual trust.

The second stage is where they will be exploring what the issues are that are to be addressed. These may change as the relationship progresses, and it is wise not to jump in too quickly in determining them so that other issues get overlooked.

The third stage can be recognised by having agreed on a plan of action that is being followed and having momentum in the learner's progress. This stage is where boredom or complacency can set in and the mentor or coach will need to be vigilant ensuring that their learner is being sufficiently challenged.

The final stage and fourth stage can often be overlooked but is important in marking the end of the relationship. This can be negative for the mentor or coach who can feel unwanted or the learner who may feel rejected or abandoned. The coach or mentor needs to be aware of signs of independence and increased confidence in their learner indicating that the end of the relationship is imminent, or it may be dictated by the imposed timescales. Either way it is important for the participants to be aware of these stages although during the support workshops more emphasis can be laid on how to deal with these situations or feelings.

Action planning will also be a part of this session, including a reminder that SMART* goals will need to be negotiated with their learner. For those who are unfamiliar with the acronym this can be easily demonstrated. How to give and receive feedback will also be an essential part of the process. It should be highlighted however that this process is not carried out in the same way as it might be in the workplace where goals are set by a manager. Feedback should always be given bearing in mind that self-esteem is not to be destroyed in the learner and that in coaching/mentoring feedback it is a two-way process. Every mentor and coach should periodically ask for feedback from his or her learner. Negative feedback should always be acknowledged, discussed with the learner if it is deemed to be unfair, and where possible implemented.

---

*Specific, Measurable, Attainable, Realistic, Time-bound

18. Feedback

This is a short solutions focussed exercise allowing the participants to extract positive things from negative dialogue and to feed that back to their partner. In pairs (A & B) they are asked to tell their partners about something that they find very irritating. This might be anything from people littering in the streets to a particular work colleague who continually fails to contribute to the rest of the team. The partner listens sympathetically and is allowed to ask further questions to find out more about the situation and why they find it so annoying. Once the speaker has exhausted the topic and fully explained, the listener should then give her or him positive feedback. In the case of the colleague who lets others down, for example, the speaker may be complimented on his or her patience and understanding and on not yet having reported the offender to the Head of the Department. This can be good practice for when they might be matched with a learner who is very negative about their situation and is failing to see anything from a more positive perspective.

19. Preparing for the First Session

This can be a simple exercise to highlight the fact that the learners may be quite apprehensive about being matched with a mentor or coach and how they might put them at ease in their first meeting. It is also a suitable time to point out that it is not particularly good practice to tell them very much about their learner prior to being matched. It is their responsibility to find out everything they need to know as part of the process of building rapport. It is a good idea to discuss practicalities such as what resources they might need such as a notepad.

Asking them to put themselves in the position of the learner will make them more aware of how to prepare for their first session. Devising some good questions in small groups to ask at the first meeting such as 'What prompted you to apply for a mentor?' or 'What expectation do you have for the coaching programme?' is also a good idea.

20. Mentor and Coach Promotion

The previous exercise will also lead nicely into this session which is about how they will be portrayed to the potential learners. Where possible it is always best to give learners a choice as to whom they work with and this can be easily achieved using mentor or coach profiles. If your plan is for the learners to select their own coach or mentor then each of your participants will need to have a profile. More information on building mentor profiles can be found in Chapter 7.

A good way to convey the need for an appropriate profile is to show some examples of poor profiles. This could be one with a very stern photograph or one of a very glamorous, heavily made-up female coach. A discussion could ensue about what 'message' this might give potential learners when they are making their selection.

The wording too is very important and again examples of poor wording can be shown. Things to avoid are sounding too bossy or opinionated, e.g. *'I have achieved great success in the field of engineering and will direct you to apply to the best organisations so you too can achieve similar success'.* Sounding too condescending can also be off-putting for potential learners. *'I know that the first few weeks at university is very tough, having been there myself, but I enjoy listening to other people's problems so can help you through this difficult time'* is unlikely to be attractive to potential learners. The more honest coaches and mentors are in their profiles, the more likely the matches will be to work well.

It is possible to give the participants sufficient time to complete the profiles within the session, although it is best to spend a good deal of time on this. It often works better, having given them some guidelines, to allow them to send their profiles to you by an agreed date. It is often a good idea to accompany this session by giving them a hand-out on tips for writing their profile to refer to later. If using one of the mentor/coach matching software licences, these guidelines for writing an attractive profile should be included in the costs.

21. Coaching and Mentoring Tools

The coaching and mentoring tools that you provide as examples for your participants will depend greatly on the aims and objectives for your programme. For example, if your programme is to support students who are re-sitting modules in a higher education environment, then the tools will consist of revision timetables, planning, and prioritising activities. Should the programme be aimed at helping higher education students into employment, then CV building tools will be required.

Some tools and models are universally useful for mentoring and coaching whatever the agenda, and these would be ones such as a SWOT analysis (Strengths, Weaknesses, Opportunities and Threats) as seen in Figure 6.1, or Whitmore's (2002) GROW model (Goals, Reality, Opportunities, and Wrap-Up).

Copyright restrictions will obviously need to be adhered to when reproducing these resources, and it is suggested that within the training some examples are shown of some particularly relevant ones and the participants are directed to websites where they can access many others such as www.businessballs.com. There are also a number of good publications in which these tools can be accessed, such as Jenny Rogers (2004), a coaching skills handbook, or Alison Hall (2008) on the S-Factor.

It is likely for educational support that your own institution will have resources available on the intranet that your participants can access.

Strengths (e.g. things you are good at, skills you already have)	**Weaknesses** (e.g. things you need to improve, skills you don't have)
• • •	• • •
Opportunities (e.g. advantages of studying your course)	**Threats** (e.g. things that might stop you from utilising the opportunities you have)
• • •	• • •

Figure 6.1 An Example of a SWOT Analysis

Some other activities such as completion of a VAK questionnaire (Visual, Auditory, and Kinaesthetic) can be useful in getting to know a learner better. It can be pointed out that knowing their own preference for learning and those of their learner, a coach or mentor can adopt methods that best suit their learner's preference. For example using 'flash cards' for revision would be more appropriate for a kinaesthetic learner than an auditory learner who is likely to benefit more from listening to tapes/lecture recordings. A coach or mentor can sometimes tend towards adopting the methods that best suit themselves and so this activity can help prevent that from happening.

There are some other useful tools that can serve very well within coaching or mentoring sessions such as Schein's careers anchors (1990) or Honey & Mumford's learning styles (2006), which are particularly useful within an employment or working context. There is a usually a cost attached for the licence to these which your institution may already have so it would be worth checking if this is available to you or your participants.

Rosenberg's Measure of Self-Esteem (1965) can also be useful in determining levels of confidence in specific areas which can then lead on to the focus of the sessions. It is extremely important to point out that the tools and activities should only be used in complete agreement with the learner and that the activity should stop if the learner appears to be feeling uncomfortable. The tools should also not be used prescriptively and only when they are appropriate for a specific situation. Some learners will very much enjoy and benefit from using these activities, but others will prefer to simply have discussions and conversation.

There are other tools such as 'good and bad points' or 'how others see me' which can often be helpful for a learner who is perhaps having trouble with some of his or her relationships such as with peers or an employer. These often allow the learner to see things from someone else's perspective which can be the first step towards improvement. Tools such as Jenny Roger's 'Empty Chair' exercise should only be used once a good rapport has been established, as the issues revealed can become quite personal or emotional.

A decision-making grid as can be seen in Figure 6.2 can be very helpful for a learner who needs to make a decision but is unsure of which direction to follow. This simple exercise allows each possible route to be explored, with the coach or mentor asking hypothetical questions to help determine what the possible outcome might be if the learner selected that particular option. An example of how they might be used can be shown on a Powerpoint slide as follows:

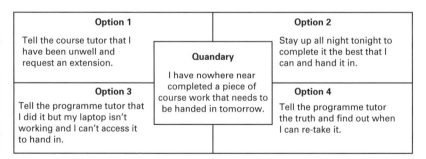

Figure 6.2 Example of a Decision-Making Grid

The tools are not particularly 'rocket science' but they do allow a learner to carefully consider all aspects of any difficulty and overcome any feeling of being overwhelmed or panicking. Once a course of action has been decided, then the coach's or mentor's role is to help the learner to set deadlines incorporating SMART targets.

The coaches and mentors should be encouraged to be as imaginative as they can with the tools, always taking into account the preferences of their learner. It may be that they have a learner who is feeling overwhelmed with all the work and assignments that she or he needs to do over the next couple of months. If you have already established that this learner has a preference for kinaesthetic methods, then you might suggest that she or he write down on cards all the tasks that she or he needs to do. Once they are all written down the learner can put them into separate piles such as 'fairly urgent', 'can wait until next month', or 'needs to be done immediately'. This can help put all the tasks into priority order and you can then move onto planning a diary allowing time for each of the tasks.

22. Applying Tools to Common Issues

Once you have demonstrated and shown Powerpoint slides of some of the tools that can be used in the programme, then the participants should be asked to re-visit the 'common issues' from exercise 16. In small groups they can be given one or two scenarios (depending on the number of participants) and asked to explore each scenario further. In their groups they should think of at least one mentoring or coaching tool that could be used in that particular scenario and suggest a SMART target that could be agreed with the learner. Once each group has noted these answers they can feed back their ideas to the rest of the group explaining how they would implement their selected tools.

For the common issue of a learner who persistently arrives late for meetings, they could consider setting the SMART goal that the learner is no later than five minutes to their meeting next week. The long-term aim would be arriving on time for all subsequent meetings. Tools that could be used in this scenario could be a prioritising tool (if they appear to be very busy) or perhaps to help plan their diary to ensure that they are leaving sufficient time for all they need to do. It is usually helpful to the participants to walk around the groups as they are working to assist them with this exercise, as they will likely be unfamiliar with the tools and how to apply them in this type of context. Rather than simply tell them what tools could be suitable, ask appropriate questions to guide them in this process, such as 'What outcome would you be aiming to achieve in this case?'

23. Real Play

Although a number of people have an inherent dislike of role play, engaging in 'real play' can be a far superior learning experience. In role play it can sometimes be most important to the participants to act the allocated part in their given scenario well, and it can seem rather contrived. On the other hand, in 'real play' each participant is asked to think of a real issue or aspect of their life that they would like to improve (with which they don't mind having a mini-coaching or mentoring session). This could be anything from being better prepared for exams to getting on better with a flat-mate or having a better work/life balance. For obvious reasons and given time constraints, it should not be an issue of a particularly serious nature. In triads each person takes the role of either the mentor (or coach), the learner, and an observer. The mentor or coach should conduct a mini-coaching or mentoring session with the learner on the topic of his or her choice whilst the observer takes notes.

After each session the observer should feed back to the mentor or coach her or his observations, of course bearing in mind the proper guidelines for giving feedback learned in the earlier session. Reflection sheets can be provided for this purpose to guide them to observe the important aspects of the communication and dialogue. Observer reflection sheets could ask the following prompts:

▶ *In which way/s did the mentor or coach set the right tone and create a comfortable atmosphere?*
▶ *How did the mentor or coach build rapport with his or her mentee?*
▶ *What messages were conveyed by the mentor's or coach's body language?*
▶ *Which questions were most effective in encouraging her or his learner to explore the issues?*
▶ *Which questions were least effective in encouraging his or her learner to explore the issues?*
▶ *How did the mentor or coach demonstrate that she or he was listening actively?*
▶ *Did the mentor or coach use any mentoring or coaching tools, and if so, how appropriate were they for the given situation?*
▶ *Was any action planning agreed and/or SMART targets set, and were those appropriate for the given situation?*

Each of the participants should take a turn in each of the roles. The trainer should observe the mini-sessions whilst remaining as unobtrusive as possible, perhaps helping to prompt the observer feedback.

The learners too should also be given the opportunity to comment on the feedback as it may be that they disagree on some aspects. This is an extremely valuable exercise, allowing the participants to practise the skills in a safe environment. Some group feedback at the end covering some of the more general aspects might also be valuable.

24. Assessment

As mentioned previously, it is worthwhile to include a short assessment exercise to check the learning and understanding of your participants. This should not be lengthy, and the given scenarios should be reasonably pertinent to your specific programme. Typical examples of an assessment scenario would be:

Example 1
Stephen, who is a very conscientious student, has been assigned some group study work which is to be handed in within the next three weeks. The others in his allocated group are contributing very little and often do not attend the arranged meetings. He has asked for your support in dealing with this, as he feels that it is unfair that he is doing most of the work but the group as a whole will be marked for the assignment.

▶ What questions might you ask?
▶ What course of action might you take?
▶ What coaching or mentoring tools or resources might you use?
▶ What targets/goals might you agree on with Stephen?

Example 2
Jasmine is finding her higher education course difficult. She has a number of deadlines approaching but has also been asked by her employer to work extra hours due to a member of staff being off sick. She has agreed targets with you previously over the last five mentoring sessions but has completed hardly any of them, putting the blame on her busy life.

▶ What questions might you ask?
▶ What course of action might you take?
▶ What coaching or mentoring tools or resources might you use?
▶ What targets/goals might you agree on with Jasmine?

Participants work individually, selecting just one of the given scenarios writing down their answers and handing them in after 20 minutes or so. These will be marked later using pre-determined marking criteria. It can be very useful to have two trainers mark the assessments independently for comparison to ensure fairness. Marks should be awarded for the quality of questions asked, the course of action, the innovative and appropriate use of the mentoring or coaching tools or resources, and the quality and appropriateness of the suggested targets/goals.

It is useful to set a minimum mark that you would allow, knowing what the maximum marks could be. For example, awarding a possible 4 marks for each of the four categories would result in a maximum score of 16. An acceptable pass mark might be between 8 and 10. You would hope that each participant would not score lower than 2 on any category.

If there are any borderline participants you might wish to invite them to a meeting where you inform them where they have not answered as you had wished and direct them to read more on that particular topic. It may be that after this conversation and feedback they will have acquired a better understanding of the requirements and you will be sufficiently confident to allow them to take part. Any who have given extremely poor answers are best not included on your programme but of course should be given appropriate feedback.

25. Plenary

The plenary session should be used to inform your participants what they should expect next. This should include the date by which they will hear whether they have passed the assessment and when they are likely to be matched. They might also be reminded of the need to provide a profile to be used for matching and given a date by when this should be submitted if you are using them.

It is also the opportune time to re-visit the post-it notes that they wrote in session three of the training. If the training has gone according to plan, then it is likely that all the concerns will have been addressed (such as worries about what to do if their learners tell them something that is upsetting them and the mentor or coach feels out of their depth). A common concern is having sufficient time to take part, and it would be prudent at this stage to remind them of the commitment and suggest that if they are still concerned it would be better to withdraw now rather than when they have been matched.

It would be hoped that not too much time elapses between the end of the training and their being matched with a learner to avoid dwindling enthusiasm. It should be explained, though, that this is not totally within your control and is dependent on people applying for support. They should be reassured that failure to match them quickly is by no means a reflection on them but is more likely to be because a suitable match for their experience or expertise has not been found.

In some case the next steps will be for the mentors or coaches to create their own profile using the ementoring platform that you have provided. If this is the case, then it is essential to ensure that they are aware of what they need to do and how to do it and also have a timeframe in which to do it. It may be that with the ementoring software that you are providing the mentees will select the mentor of their choice using the profiles, and so non-completion of a profile will result in their not being selected.

▶ Online training

The above schedule is ideal for classroom-based training; however it may be that for geographical or other reasons classroom-based training is not feasible. Online training in these circumstances may be an option. Whilst the same activities will not all be possible, the format for the training should remain the same. It can be presented through multiple choice questions and case studies. The assessment process should still be feasible if using an appropriate platform that allows for the answers to be checked by the coordinator.

A useful format would be to split the training into separate sections. It would be prudent for participants to complete each section systematically and correctly before being permitted to move onto the next. Each set of questions should be preceded by some reading material provided either online or through a resources pack. The sections could be as follows:

Section 1 - Introduction to the mentoring or coaching programme
This should cover the aims and objectives for the mentoring or coaching programme as well as the skills required to be a successful mentor or coach.

Section 2 - Effective questioning
In the same way as the classroom-based training, participants should be introduced to the different question types and be allowed to practice rephrasing questions. They should also be able to identify poor questions for a mentoring or coaching context.

Section 3 - Building rapport
Participants can be introduced to different communication styles and ways in which to build rapport effectively. The listening skills questionnaire can be introduced to give them an awareness of areas where they need to develop.

Section 4 - Preparing for the first session
This section should be used to introduce the participants to the idea of contracting with their allocated learner. It should also cover the first contact, meeting expectations, and appropriate ways to send an introductory email or prepare for a face-to-face meeting as appropriate to your programme. This section could also include directions for building their profile.

Section 5 - Conducting mentoring or coaching sessions
This section should cover the phases of mentoring and how to recognise each of them. It should also contain details on giving and receiving feedback as well as action planning and the importance of setting SMART targets.

Section 6 - Challenging and tackling difficult issues

In this section some of the more common issues should be tackled such as learners who are not engaged with the programme, those who persistently blame others for their failings, or those who lack focus or have multiple issues.

Section 7 - Case study questions

Mentoring or coaching tools specific to your programme should be introduced at this stage with similar case studies to those used in the classroom-based training. As with the final assessment used in the classroom-based training, participants should be asked to consider the given case studies and provide comprehensive answers on appropriate questions to ask, SMART targets, appropriate action, and the implementation of the tools.

Whilst mentoring and coaching are very human interventions and therefore better suit classroom-based training, online training can be appropriate. This is particularly true when the mentoring programme is to provide more functional rather than emotional support. If the programme is to be conducted entirely through electronic means, then this makes an even stronger case for online as opposed to classroom-based training.

7 Mentee/Coachee Recruitment and Matching

Promotion of the scheme to mentees or coachees should be conducted in a similar way to mentor and coach recruitment. It should be tailored to the aims and objectives of the particular programme. Extra care should be taken when the programme is targeting those from disadvantaged groups such as students with a disability or from low-income backgrounds so as not to patronise or demean them. The scheme will need to be promoted in a positive way.

If, for example you are targeting students who are underachieving, then you would not draw attention to this in your promotional literature. It could be advertised as described in Box 7.1.

Box 7.1 Example of Coachee Promotion

Interested in taking the next step to success?
We can link you with a trained peer coach who can help you achieve the results you want.

Are there aspects of your course that you are finding more challenging?

▶ You may want to achieve a better grade
▶ Improve your essay writing or presentation skills
▶ Improve your revision or time management techniques
▶ Perhaps you had to do re-sits
▶ Do you need to be re-motivated?

One of our trained student coaches could help you achieve your goal/s whether that is obtaining a 1st, becoming better prepared for exams, or producing 'top graded' coursework. Peer Coaches will be successful students on track for at least a 2:1.

Contact can be via email or face to face depending on what you and your coach decide and your coach can work with you for a period of 10 weeks.

Contact the administrator for more details or for an application form.

A programme aimed at supporting the integration of students from a lower socioeconomic background into higher education might be promoted with a presentation using phrases such as those seen in Box 7.2.

Box 7.2 Example of Mentee Recruitment for Underachieving Students

> Why Mentoring?
> Research has shown that students who receive mentoring are:
>
> ▶ More likely to complete their degree
> ▶ Attain higher grades
> ▶ Find the student experience more fulfilling

If you have some quotes from previous participants then use them in your presentation. Examples of quotes should give a variety of practical reasons why it was helpful, as seen in Figure 7.1, rather than just stating bland benefits such as *'my mentor was really helpful'*.

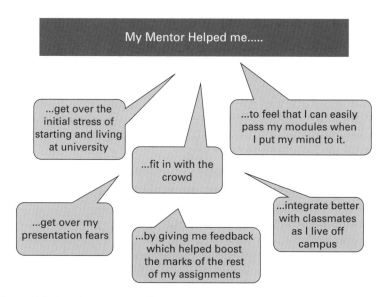

Figure 7.1 Genuine Mentee Evaluation Quotes

Potential learners should also be informed who the mentors are likely to be and given reassurance that they have been properly selected, recruited, and trained. For example, let them know that the criterion was for them to have two years' experience in the workplace or be achieving at least a 2:1. It is worth mentioning that they will be supported by a mentoring or coaching coordinator.

As part of the promotional materials potential learners should also be informed of what to expect from their mentor using phrases such as:

Mentors will:

▶ Encourage and support you
▶ Listen
▶ Answer questions
▶ Ask questions that will help you to make your own decisions
▶ Give feedback
▶ Respect confidentiality

Potential learners should also be informed about how to apply and reminded of their commitment to the relationship, such as responding promptly to emails and turning up on time to meetings. It is worthwhile reminding them that it is they who will set the agenda for the sessions according to their needs.

It might be worth producing an FAQ sheet for your programme, such as the one in Box 7.3 for an academic peer-mentoring scheme, which will serve as another reminder for the parameters of the programme. The details will of course need to be adapted to suit your particular scheme.

Box 7.3 Example of a Mentee FAQ Sheet

Mentoring Programme FAQs

How could seeing a mentor help?
Mentors are there to proactively help you achieve your full academic potential and make the most of your time at University. They could help with a particular aspect of your studies that you are finding difficult or help with matters such as managing your time better, choosing the right modules for you or perhaps to just stay motivated. Sometimes peer support can be more helpful than that from a member of staff.

Is my mentor trained?
Yes, all peer mentors have had appropriate training and passed the selection process. Mentors volunteer their time to help support others and some hope to develop their own communication skills by taking part. All will currently be successful students and have studied at the University for at least a year, as this is part of the selection process.

How often will I communicate with a mentor?
You and your mentor can decide what will suit you both, but a guideline might be one hourly meeting every week or a couple of emails per week. You might adapt the frequency according to your needs.

What if my mentor is unable to meet with me?

The Ementoring system allows you to communicate with your mentor via email if for geographical reasons or time constraints you are unable to meet face to face.

What will my mentor be like?

Peer mentors come in all shapes and sizes but will be successfully studying at the University. Before matching you with a mentor the scheme coordinator will arrange to talk to you with the aim of pairing you with a mentor with whom you will hopefully get on well and have something in common.

How do we know we will get on, and what if we don't?

The scheme coordinator will give careful consideration at the outset to matching you with your mentor and you will be involved in the selection process. The coordinator will also be available throughout for you to talk to about any problems that arise, and they will also be in touch with you both from time to time to find out how things are going. If things still don't work out, it may be possible to match you with someone else.

Will I then be offered another mentor?

The coordinator will try to accommodate you but this is subject to another suitable mentor being available.

How are we matched?

Attempts will be made to match your stated needs with that of the mentor's strengths and expertise. Hobbies might also be taken into account and the type of course and modules that you are both studying. However, this is not an exact science; it will depend on mentor availability and it cannot be guaranteed that your mentor will be studying exactly the same course as you. Profiles are available so that you can select the mentor that you would prefer to work with.

Does anyone else have access to your emails?

Software will be in place that will monitor the frequency of the email contact. This will enable us, along with your (and your mentor's) feedback to fully evaluate the efficacy of the scheme. This software does allow the coordinator **only** to access the emails if necessary, but this will not be carried out routinely.

What do I need to do next?

Contact mentoradministrator@email.com in the Mentoring Department for an application/profile form. An appointment will be made for you to discuss any worries or thoughts you have with the Mentoring Coordinator. Alternatively, you can hand in the completed form at the office.

It will be necessary to ensure that your learners know what is expected of them prior to being matched with one of your mentors or coaches. It is worthwhile that they also complete an application or profile form which has the dual purpose of providing valuable information for the matching process. Completing an application form and attending an induction session demonstrates their motivation to be involved. Those who do not take the time to complete an application form or turn up for an induction session are more likely to show the same lack of motivation if matched with a mentor or coach.

An example of a mentee/application or profile form can be found in Appendix 5. These questions can be changed to suit the particular scheme. It would also be advisable to include some pre-intervention questions to enable a thorough evaluation of the programme. Further information on evaluation can be found in Chapter 10.

Particularly where your mentors are not plentiful in numbers, it is import-ant not to waste their time with a learner who is not fully engaged. The objective is to have participants who are motivated and sufficiently proactive to arrange their own meetings without too much of your intervention. Another important factor in setting the process off to a good start is the involvement of the learner in the coach or mentor selection process.

▶ **Utilising Mentor or Coach Profiles**

Where possible there should be coach or mentor profiles available. These do not need to be overloaded with information but should contain some details such as what the coaches/mentors are studying (or have studied, if alumni). The profiles could contain details of the optional modules selected (if they are higher education students), something about their hobbies and a short piece of text detailing what they can offer as a mentor or coach. This should be appropriate to the aims and objectives of your scheme. For example, if it is an academic peer-coaching programme, then they might state that they are particularly strong in essay writing or research skills. They should also detail in what year of study they are and any work experience. For business mentors (supporting final-year students into work) it will be necessary for them to detail their career and industry experience.

It is always wise to include a photograph on the profile, although it should be an appropriate one. It should be neither too formal nor informal and not one that has a serious expression such as in a passport photograph. The idea is to appear professional but friendly and approachable. The difference a photograph can make has been shown from experience. One mentor who had used an expressionless passport photograph on his profile was continually overlooked by prospective mentees. Once the photograph was changed, he became very much in demand without changing any of the text. Those with friendly smiles are likely to be selected more frequently.

▶ Guidelines for Writing Profiles

Remember that learners will be browsing the profiles so bear this in mind and ensure that they are attractive from their viewpoint. Ensure that the support being offered is what they might seek from their coach or mentor. It is important that mentors or coaches have integrity. For example, humour can be included in a profile but only if that is the coach's or mentor's usual style.

It is wise to use just a first name (or the name that the coach or mentor prefers to be called) to avoid learners contacting them directly through social media.

Including the town or county where they reside/originate can be useful as some students like to be matched with someone who originates from the same location.

If including an age, then it is more practical to use a date of birth so that this doesn't date. In some programmes you may have a mixture of younger and more mature mentors and this could be a major factor in the learner selection process. It would be more common for a mature learner to request a more mature coach or mentor.

If it is a higher education peer-mentoring scheme then the coach or mentor will need to specify whether he or she is a postgraduate or undergraduate student. It is likely that prospective learners will want to know details of their first degree as well as their current course. It might even be appropriate to include optional modules and possibly grades attained, particularly if the support being offered is of an academic nature. It will be important to specify the year of study so that the learners can make their choice. It will help to clarify precise details such as being in their fourth and final year of undergraduate study, having completed a work placement in the previous year, or having changed courses or repeated a year.

Employment details can be left blank if there has been no employment that is significant. However an employment record or voluntary work that might be of interest to learners, such as working within the NHS Trust or in a particular business sector, is worth including.

Obviously with an Alumni, Career, or Business Mentoring programme the employment section will be very significant and a resume of the mentor's or coach's career path will be required. However it should only highlight particular areas and organisations that will be of interest to the learners.

There may be other details that would be important to include for your particular programme. This might be languages spoken if you are working with international students or on a bilingual mentoring scheme.

Interests should not be exaggerated in order to show off, but some potential learners are attracted to a coach or mentor who shares the same music preferences and interests. It can also help as an icebreaker to have shared hobbies.

One of the most important parts of the profile is the section on what your participants can offer as a coach or mentor. It should be relatively brief, not a monologue, and should bear in mind the following points:

- ▶ Not exceed 100 words
- ▶ Written naturally, using the mentor's or coach's normal vocabulary
- ▶ Free of typos and abbreviations
- ▶ Stating strengths honestly (e.g. 'I have acquired some useful tips for revision and exam preparation that I am willing to share')
- ▶ Learners are keen to work with high-achieving coaches, so modesty about achievements should be spared (e.g. 'I am the youngest Senior Manager within the organisation')
- ▶ Rather than talk about possible issues that they can support with, refer to what the mentor or coach can do for them (e.g. 'I can motivate you to achieve higher grades and can help you plan and structure assignments')
- ▶ No false promises (e.g. 'I will ensure that I am available whenever you need support')

▶ Matching Events

These can be useful and will certainly result in a robust matching process. However they can be more problematic to arrange if you have a number of participants who are external to the university. They are also likely to result in additional expenses if you are reimbursing external mentors for their travel costs.

However, if funds allow and it is practicable to host an event, it should result in an easier matching process. A variety of methods can be adopted to integrate the mentors and coaches with the learners. An advantage is that you can induct the learners at the same time with the mentors present. This way all participants can gain a shared understanding of the mentoring or coaching process. It is worth noting, though, that with a single event it would not be feasible to incorporate the mentor or coach training. This would have to be held on a separate occasion. With careful planning you may be able to finish the mentor or coach training session and add the matching event at the end of the second day, thereby avoiding the need to invite them in again.

Matching events can be of a relatively short duration and will consist mainly of an introductory reminder of the aims and objectives for the programme. An activity or two would be useful as long as they are designed to integrate both the mentors/coaches and the learners. This could be a speed matching type arrangement where each mentor/coach has a minute to speak to a learner. Mentors/coaches sit in a line opposite a similar line of the mentees/coaches. Participants can be instructed to find out two facts about the person sitting in front of them until the end is signalled and they have to move onto the next person. This continues until they arrive back in their original starting position.

It is also possible to split the participants into mixed groups of learners and coaches and set them group tasks. This will promote conversation and team working, allowing them to find out more about each other. The nature of the activities will need to be age appropriate. For young children, for example, a group task could be to build the tallest structure using only marshmallows and uncooked spaghetti or an origami activity. For adults it would be more appropriate to have a puzzle or quiz of some sort. As long as the tasks are enjoyable and promote conversation and mixing of the groups, they will serve their purpose.

Once the activities are over, each learner is asked to list three of the mentors/coaches they would prefer to work with. Alternatively you could ask them to name any that they would not wish to work with. Being given this choice, it is very rare in my experience for the learners to decline the opportunity of working with any one of the mentors/coaches. Surprisingly it is also unusual for any of the participants to remain unmatched following an event such as this. This method also has the bonus of allowing the learner's choice in whom they work with which invariably sets the relationship off to a good start.

You will find that people who are suited will generally gravitate towards each other and the matching process will become quite simple thereafter. Observing these activities closely is also recommended as much information can be gleaned from the body language of the participants. An example of this was when a shy young man made little if no eye contact when a female mentor was seated opposite him in the speed matching. However when a male mentor sat opposite him he was drawn into more animated conversation. It was apparent that a male mentor in his case would be a better match.

▶ Coordinator Matching

There are various methods of matching your participants as a paper-based exercise. The more information collected on the application or profile form, the better chance you will have of making a good match. If it is not possible to allow the learners to select their own mentor or coach, then you can set criteria for the matching. This could be anything from course studied, year of study, the employment sector of interest, to geographical location. These criteria can be prioritised and the learners matched according to coach or mentor availability. Shared interests could also be factored into the decision if there appear to be no other commonalities.

Whilst this is not a scientific exercise, there is no need for anxiety if your mentors or coaches have been well prepared for the role. A well-trained mentor or coach will be able to build rapport and have the skills to work with any learner, adapting to their needs.

The following case study demonstrates the need for a robust mentee induction to ensure that the participants are fully engaged.

CASE STUDY 4
Business Career Mentoring Programme (Australia)

Name of institution: University of Western Australia

Name of programme: Career Mentor Link and Women in Engineering (www.careermentorlink.uwa.edu.au)

Number of years that the programme has been delivered:
Perth programme since 2003, Singapore programme since 2010, Women in Engineering since 2014

Number of mentors: Varies each year but over 380 in 2015

Number of mentees: Varies each year but over 430 in 2015

Who is supported:
The Perth programme is open to any currently enrolled student at UWA who has completed at least first year of an undergrad degree. The Singapore programme is open to final-year current students who are from Singapore, studying in Perth and, returning home to Singapore at the end of their degree and to students who are going on Exchange to Singapore during the programme.

The Women in Engineering programme is open to female students who are enrolled in either a Bachelor of Engineering or Master of Professional Engineering course.

How the need was identified:
Through talking to students it was clear that they needed a mechanism to have access to industry professionals in order to supplement their academic learning. Not all courses at UWA have a practicum or work placement component so mentoring is an excellent way for students to start developing their industry networks and exploring career options.

Students need to be currently enrolled at UWA and have completed at least the first year of an undergraduate degree. They need to complete an Expression of Interest form, attend an Information session and submit a résumé and registration form. There is no minimum grade requirement.

Who are the mentors:
Mentors in the programme are industry professionals generally with at least four years' work experience.

The aims/objectives for the mentoring:
The main aim of the programme is to help students develop the skills they need to manage their career. It's not about work experience: the role of the mentor is to guide, support and encourage the mentee while they explore career options, learn new skills such as networking, practise skills such as interview skills and résumé writing, and/or make the transition to employment at the end of their degree.

The definition/model of mentoring that is adopted:
Mentoring is generally on a one-to-one basis although occasionally a mentor will be matched with two mentees. Most contact between mentors and mentees is face to face, but Skype and email are also used, particularly in the Singapore programme. All participants are provided with a manual and guidelines for the programme and there are some minimum requirements (e.g. monthly catch-ups and a progress report halfway through), but other than this the programme is designed to be as flexible as possible to enable participants to get the most out of it.

How suitable mentors are selected and recruited:
For the Perth programme, preference is given to mentors living in Western Australia (but this is not essential), and they need to have at least four years' work experience. For the Singapore programme, the mentors must be living in Singapore, ideally be UWA alumni, and have at least four years' work experience.

Both the Perth and Singapore programmes have a high percentage of returning mentors each year (the Perth programme has some mentors who have been involved since 2004). New mentors are recruited using alumni communication channels (newsletters, emails) and employer contacts through the Careers Centre. The largest group however are found through asking existing mentors to spread the word to their colleagues and networks.

The duration of the mentoring relationships:
The Perth and Women in Engineering programmes begin in April and the Singapore programme begins in June.

The mentor training plan:
All mentors receive a PDF manual. There is an introductory session aimed at new mentors in March delivered by the programme coordinator. Other training opportunities are offered, e.g. Coaching skills, Understanding Cultural Diversity. These are delivered by appropriate facilitators.

The mentee induction process:
Mentees must complete an online Expression of Interest form, attend an Information Session, and submit a registration form and a copy of their résumé.

Matching criteria and process:
Mentors and mentees are matched manually by the coordinator based on employment details and expertise of the mentor and studies and career goals of the mentees.

Frequency of the meetings:
The minimum requirement is that mentors and mentees catch up at least once per month during the programme. At least two of the catch-ups must be face to face but the others can be via emails, phone, or Skype. Locations and times of the meetings are decided by the participants. A number of events are held during the Perth programme and an annual networking event for the Singapore programme to provide participants with a chance to meet up.

How the mentors are supported:
Regular emails are sent out to all mentors including 'Mentoring tips'. Training opportunities are provided (e.g. Coaching Skills, Understanding Cultural Diversity). Mentor contact details have been circulated within the group so that all mentors can contact other mentors directly if required.

The Mentoring Coordinator role:
There is a programme coordinator who is employed three days per week (0.6 FTE) to run all three programmes.

Funding arrangements:
The coordinator's position is funded by UWA. The other costs of the programme are funded through sponsorship from industry partners and money from the Student Services and Amenities Fee (SSAF).

Evaluation arrangements:
Students are required to submit a progress report halfway through the programme. Both mentors and mentees are asked to complete an evaluation form at the end of the programme. Completion is compulsory for mentees and voluntary for mentors. Both mentors and mentees are asked about the effectiveness of the programme.

Major obstacles in setting up the programme:
Participant numbers have continually grown across all programmes since they began. The biggest issue is trying to ensure that the mentees' expectations are aligned with the programme and that the mentees remained engaged. Engagement appears to be an issue particularly with the Singapore programme where much of the contact is via Skype and email.

How these are overcome:
The three-step registration process for the students was set up in order to try to ensure the commitment level of the students registering for the programme. This has had some success.

Events are held throughout the length of the Perth and Women in Engineering programmes in order to keep participants engaged. Participants in the Singapore programme who are based in Perth are also invited to these events.

Careful attention is paid to matching of mentees and mentors wherever possible. While many mentors feel comfortable mentoring a wide variety of students, experience has shown that students need to feel that a match is relevant to their studies and career aspirations in order to engage.

Programme recommendations:
Each programme has been modified slightly over the years based on feedback from participants. Both are well established and likely to continue on an on-going basis.

▶ Matching Using Software

There are a number of software packages available to assist with the matching process that can be extremely helpful, particularly where there are a large number of applicants. Whilst it is not appropriate for this text to recommend any particular package, it would be prudent to advise a full exploration of the facilities each of them offers before purchasing any. These packages can be costly and will also require a contract of at least one year, making mistakes expensive.

The facilities offered can vary from making the matches for you based upon set criteria to merely creating profiles for the participants so that they can select their own preferences. Some even provide resources that can be accessed by your participants, particularly for employability- and career-based mentoring programmes. There are even software packages designed for young people, providing resources to help them select career paths and appropriate higher education courses.

Many of these packages are dependent on the participants using the facilities provided. The coordinator role will therefore become one of chasing up and supporting the participants to fully utilise and access the software effectively.

Which method to use to match your participants will depend on the numbers involved and the availability of your coaches and mentors. You may have to hold more than one matching event to accommodate everyone and it may be possible to implement more than one of these methods. It may be that in your pilot programme a manual matching process is feasible, but as the numbers grow it may be more appropriate to purchase software to aid the process. It is however always prudent, when obtaining feedback from your participants, to ask how satisfied they were with the matching process. This will enable you to monitor the efficacy of any system that you are using and the possible need to improve it.

The Pride Mentoring Programme case study shows how the matching process evolved as a result of participant feedback.

CASE STUDY 5
Pride Mentoring Programme for LGBTIQ students

Name of institution: RMIT University

Name of programme: Pride Mentoring Programme

Number of years that the programme has been delivered: Since 2012 (on-going)

Number of matches:
One-to-one mentoring:
2015 – 41 partnerships created (until August 2015)
2014 – 47 partnerships
2013 – 45 partnerships
2012 – 12 partnerships during the pilot programme

Who is supported:
This programme supports Lesbian, Gay, Bisexual, Transgender, Intersex, and Queer or Questioning (LGBTIQ) students at RMIT University. Students

range from being out to most people and comfortable with their sexuality and well engaged in the LGBTIQ community to being closeted, still learning to accept their sexuality, and not being engaged in the LGBTIQ community at all.

The needs of students vary from solely career development concerns to a combination of career development issues and guidance on accepting their sexuality/gender identity.

How the needs are identified:
Mentees are required to complete a registration form. This form identifies:
► students' level of education
► course they are enrolled in
► information on their gender and sexual identity
► to what degree they are out about their sexual/gender identity
► their level of involvement in the LGBTIQ community
► their reasoning for wanting to participate in the programme
► future career goals, if known
► requirements or preferences regarding the mentor they are matched with

Who are the mentors:
Mentees are supported by industry professionals (with minimum three years of managerial experience) who also identify as LGBTIQ and are out and comfortable about their sexuality/gender identity.

The aims/objectives for the mentoring:
The Pride Mentoring Programme supports RMIT lesbian, gay, bisexual, transgender, intersex, queer or questioning (LGBTIQ) students who are preparing to enter the workforce and may be faced with additional career planning challenges related to sexual orientation or gender identity.

The Pride Mentoring Programme is an opportunity for students who are exploring their sexual orientation and gender expression to receive personal support from an experienced industry professional who also identifies as LGBTIQ.

The definition/model of mentoring adopted:
Mentors are encouraged to treat the mentoring as an equal partnership and adopt a nondirective approach. This allows both the mentor and mentee to gain from the interactions. The mentoring is on a face-to-face and one-on-one basis. Mentors and mentees are also able to engage in remote mentoring (via Skype for example) for some of the meetings if required. If a mentor indicates she or he is able to take on multiple mentees, we allow this if an appropriate opportunity arises. (These are separate one-on-one mentoring partnerships, not group mentoring.)

How suitable mentors are selected and recruited:
The programme is promoted to a range of organisations via their HR or Diversity and Inclusion departments during the year to engage new mentors, with many mentors also being recruited by word of mouth from current/previous mentors. All mentors undergo a reference check and are required to have a minimum of three years' managerial experience. LGBTIQ professionals from all disciplines and sectors are welcomed.

The duration of the mentoring relationships:
The programme offers a minimum of a 12-week partnership. Partnerships are no longer semester based but can commence at any stage throughout the academic year.

The mentor induction and training plan:
An online Induction Module was developed, which all participants are required to complete prior to participation. There is a short quiz to test their understanding of the process, and completion of this is confirmed prior to participation.

Commencing in 2015, Mentor Development Sessions were established to provide mentors with an opportunity to learn from one another, network, and be presented with engaging and relevant material to assist with their mentoring experience. These sessions are voluntary and have been very well received by mentors.

The mentee induction and training process:
Mentees also complete an induction module and complete a short quiz to test their understanding of the mentoring process, their role and responsibilities prior to participation. Mentee Workshops are also run throughout the year to provide students with an opportunity to learn more about the programme, the mentoring system and for support to be offered.

Matching criteria and process:
Mentors and mentees were initially matched manually on basis of:

▶ gender/sexuality match between mentor and student
▶ student's career goals and mentor's industry experience
▶ whether the student requires more career or personal guidance and whether a mentor is willing/able to provide the required personal guidance
▶ mentors' and students' interests and hobbies

However, in 2015 an online matching system was introduced in response to participants' need to have more control over the selection of their mentor or mentee. The system enables mentors to create 'profiles' and allows the students to browse and request a particular mentor. Enabling students to select their own mentor has improved the quality of the partnerships established and the level of engagement of participants.

Frequency of meetings:
Participants are required to make a minimum time commitment of one hour per month for the duration of the partnership. Meeting times and locations are flexible, however, to suit the needs of the individuals. The introduction of mentoring software in 2015, which will be discussed later, gives mentors and mentees the capacity to engage in email exchanges, set-up meetings, and record tasks and goals.

How the mentors are supported:
Mentors have access to the RMIT mentoring team via telephone or email should they require support regarding their mentoring partnership. Mentors approach the team if their mentee is not engaging, if their mentee discloses information that the mentor is concerned about, if the mentor requires support around structuring meetings, etc. There is also a Support Services resource that provides mentors with relevant information on LGBTIQ and mental health organisations that they may pass on to their mentees.

The mentoring team role:
The programme is supported by the Careers and Employability Mentoring Team.

The time spent on coordinating the programme varies considerably. When a partnership is underway and any initial hurdles have been resolved, a partnership requires minimum support. The mentoring system sends automated messages and prompts participants to keep the partnership on track and engaged. Feedback requests are also managed by the system.

The team is also responsible for programme advertising and marketing, recruitment of students and mentors, management of participant experience, and announcements and participant communications.

At the end of the programme, participants are invited to a 'wrap-up event' to thank them and encourage future participation of mentors.

Funding arrangements:
This programme is funded by the Student Services Amenities Fee (SSAF).

Evaluation arrangements:
We require mentors and mentees to complete a mid-programme feedback form and a more extensive end of programme evaluation.

In addition to qualitative data, more recently the survey questions have been adjusted to collect more quantitative data on impact and outcomes on career development. Mentees are asked about additional opportunities provided by the industry mentors, such as workplace visits and shadowing, paid employment or internship opportunities, professional networking opportunities, and referrals.

Major obstacles in setting up the programme:
As the Pride Mentoring Programme was the first of its kind in an Australian university, there were a number of obstacles to be faced when it was first established. One such obstacle was the lack of resources to support the programme in its infancy. When the programme was first proposed, the concept of Industry Mentoring was new to RMIT's Careers Department. In 2012 the programme was developed and managed solely by Adam Rowland, Manager, Employment and Employer Services, who undertook the recruitment of participants and the programme administration, running it as a small pilot programme.

Another obstacle was the recruitment of mentors and mentees for the pilot year of the programme. The recruitment of mentors was primarily done through industry connections and word of mouth, which limited the number of participants. Recruiting student mentees was also challenging as most students were not aware of the programme, largely due to the limited resources for establishing targeted communications. In addition to this, the benefits of mentoring were generally not known by students, leading to difficulties in recruiting the first student participants.

How these were overcome:
Although the initial recruitment of mentors was challenging due to the small scope of the programme, support was quickly built for the programme by gaining industry endorsement from large multinational organisations. Organisations that were first approached regarding endorsements were those with well-developed Diversity and Inclusion policies that specifically included LGBTIQ people, for example, National Australia Bank, PriceWaterhouseCooopers, and Accenture. Further, organisations that had strong ties with the LGBTIQ community (for example, involvement with the Midsumma Festival and Melbourne Queer Film Festival) were approached and encouraged to promote participation among their employees and members.

Building these industry connections during 2012 was essential to the ultimate success of the pilot programme and ensured that the programme continued in 2013 and beyond.

The establishment of the larger Industry Mentoring Programme, which Pride Mentoring now sits under, has meant that staff resources as well as funding have increased. This has allowed for more time and effort being spent on student recruitment efforts, including targeted communications and Pride Mentoring workshops. From 2015, a dedicated staff member has been appointed to recruit and support mentors across the industry mentoring programmes at RMIT. The Pride Mentoring Programme has now entered into its fourth year and has had a total of 121 mentors from a range of industries.

Programme recommendations:

Previous programme feedback resulted in RMIT and the Victorian AIDS Council collaborating to host the Pride Employment Forum. The forum provided participants with information relating to seeking employment while still celebrating their sexuality and gender identity. In addition, the forum discussed the impact of HIV on employment, such as seeking employment and disclosure in the workplace.

In 2014, although 83% of mentors and 94% of students stated that they were satisfied with the matching process, there were many comments made regarding a desire for more involvement with the process. In view of this feedback, mentoring software was introduced in 2015 that made the matching process very transparent with much of the process being shifted to a self-matching procedure.

8 Record Keeping

To enable monitoring of the mentoring or coaching relationships, it is very useful for the participants to keep a record of each of their meetings. These can be in the form of contact logs that both the mentor/coach and the learner sign each time they meet.

These logs will serve a number of purposes including to keep both the coach/mentor and learner focussed and outcome orientated. If these are to be submitted regularly to the mentoring coordinator, it is essential that they do not contain very personal information. It should be made clear to both your learners and mentors/coaches that these will be submitted and viewed by a coordinator and as such will be an 'open document'. The general gist of the conversation only should therefore be recorded rather than a detailed account of the discussions. However the agreed actions should be quite precise.

If these are regularly submitted, they will be invaluable in helping to determine the nature of the support being given as well as the frequency of the meetings. The information that they contain will be important for inclusion in the evaluation process as they will show trends in the topics discussed between the different pairs of mentors or coaches. The participants should also be encouraged to revisit these logs regularly in order to ensure that they are alerted to the progress being made. The logs can be relatively simple, such as the one in Table 8.1.

Table 8.1 Example of a Mentor or Coach Contact Log

Session Number:	**Date:**	
Topic of Discussion		
Agreed Actions:		
By When?		
Signed	Mentor	Mentee ....

If your scheme consists of both face to face and communication by other methods such as telephone, Skype or email, the details can still be recorded via this method. Logs can be submitted electronically or they might even be incorporated as part of a mentoring software package if you have purchased one.

▶ Learning Logs

These can be extremely useful in further developing coaching and mentoring skills for your participants, encouraging reflective learning. In particular learning logs can be useful when you propose to offer some form of accreditation or certification for coaches'/mentors' contribution.

Mentors and coaches should be encouraged to complete learning logs following each session they have with their learner. Unlike the contact logs, the content of these is not shared with their learner. They are for personal development use only or utilised for partial submission of a written assignment should they be undertaking an accredited mentoring or coaching module.

The coaches and mentors should be encouraged to apply the stages of Kolb's Experiential Learning cycle to make the most of the learning opportunity.

Stage 1 – Review the experiences that they have had (reflective observation).

Stage 2 – Think about all the different meanings that they might have (abstract conceptualisation).

Stage 3 – Reach a conclusion about what they could do better/differently next time (active experimentation).

Stage 4 – Put it into action in a clear and realistic manner noting how and when they are going to do it (concrete experience).

For areas of improvement they should think of alternative ways that they could have handled a given situation or things that they might have said or asked that would have been more appropriate. It may be possible for them to revisit these issues at a later date and incorporate some of these ideas.

They should reflect on the use of mentoring or coaching tools and their appropriateness to a given situation. They could even explore alternative tools or methods that may be more appropriate for their particular learner.

Taking this systematic approach will allow them to make the most of the mentoring or coaching experience to improve their own practice. Honing mentoring and coaching skills is an on-going process, and it is essential that a number of different approaches are used. Different learners will respond differently to different techniques and approaches. An approach that doesn't work well at one stage of a relationship may be hugely successful later on once a better rapport has been achieved.

Basic questions to aid reflective learning can be as follows:

▶ What actually happened/what was the experience?
▶ What was the learning gained from this?
▶ What would I do differently or how would I react differently next time?
▶ What further support, learning, or resources would be helpful for next time?
▶ What are the next steps to improve my practice/understanding in this area?

Keeping records of meetings such as the ones suggested above will optimise the evaluation process, and if you are recompensing your mentors or coaches, it will enable you to do so in a fair and defensible manner. You will be able to calculate the number of meetings, emails and Skype contact to determine the exact level of commitment and reimburse them accordingly.

▶ Mentor or Coach Accreditation

If you are offering any form of accreditation for your mentors or coaches, then keeping detailed learning logs for each of their sessions will likely be essential practice. There are a growing number of governing bodies who are offering coaching or mentoring accreditation, and this could be something that your participants will find very valuable. If funding allows, the reward offered for being a mentor or coach may include the opportunity to receive accreditation for their efforts through one of these governing bodies. This could be expensive, but if there are substantial numbers who are being referred to them, then a significant discount could possibly be negotiated.

It may be more practical to develop an accredited module within your own institution. Many courses already include a mentoring or coaching module, particularly in nursing or in the caring professions. These modules could be adapted with relative ease or new ones written. It may be feasible to offer your mentors or coaches a choice of receiving a voucher or the opportunity of accreditation.

Whilst it is advised that you should be collecting records of contact etc. from your mentors and coaches as part of your programme, those who wish to undertake an accredited module will need to produce further evidence of their learning in this role. The learning logs suggested earlier could form part of this process although additional evidence is likely to be required. An essay on the development of their communication skills could provide additional evidence, and testimonials from learners another form of evidence.

A testimonial need not be too onerous but should provide an account of the impact that their coach or mentor has had and indicate whether good practice has been adhered to. If possible it would be prudent for each mentor or coach to provide two testimonials from different learners. An example of a testimonial can be seen in Table 8.2.

Table 8.2 Example of a Learner Testimonial

Testimonial for ....
Please comment on how your mentor/coach defined her or his role and the boundaries of your relationship.
Please comment on how your mentor/coach engaged you, progressed your relationship and helped you to identify your goals.
Please comment on the approaches and methods that your coach/mentor used within your meetings (including tools/activities etc.).
Please comment on any impact that has occurred through meeting with your mentor/coach.

The learning logs in the case of accredited mentoring or coaches will need to be completed effectually. Whilst it is good practice to complete logs routinely following each session they should not simply be 'an account' of the mentoring or coaching session/s but should demonstrate learning of the mentoring or coaching process. The logs could be used from one or more of the learners that they are working with although the anonymity of the learner should always be maintained prior to submission. This could be achieved by referring to the learner by their first name, by their initials only or by using a fictitious name. The information contained in the logs should not in any way enable the learner/s to be identified and so they should avoid using company/organisation names etc.

The following structure may be useful to write about 'key events' in learning:

Identifying a Key Event

▶ What happened?
▶ What did I notice?
▶ How did it affect me and what were my reactions?

I have deepened my understanding through...

▶ personal reflection
▶ consulting others about their perceptions of the situation
▶ drawing on the mentoring, coaching, or other literature

As a result of this reflection my new approaches are to...

▶ view the situation differently
▶ react or respond in a different way
▶ adopt a different approach or technique

It may be necessary for learners to submit a summary paragraph to accompany the logs as a way of explaining their development.

The word count for any essay etc. will depend on the level of the accredited module but, as a minimum, evidence of at least four hours of coaching or mentoring support should be presented. As with any accredited module, the level of accreditation is reflected in the number of study and practice hours.

You should be prepared for coaches and mentors who intend to undertake the accreditation process to withdraw. A clear deadline should be set not only for submission of logs but for informing you of their intention to undertake the accreditation. It is not uncommon, as time progresses and work commitments increase, for coaches and mentors to decide against undertaking this additional task. Many will have underestimated the amount of time and effort that producing this evidence of learning will take. Having clear deadlines for withdrawals etc. will ensure that no costs are outlaid unnecessarily. There will also need to be clarity around the assessment criteria, as it may be that some of the evidence presented will not meet the required standards for certification.

9 Mentor or Coach Supervision

An essential part of the process in a best practice scheme is the provision of regular supervision for your mentors and coaches. Once inducted and matched, the learners should not have to contact the coordinator unless an issue arises with their relationship or with their particular coach or mentor. However your mentors and coaches should be fully supported throughout the process. Whilst thorough training will prepare them to a degree, it is not until they are actually matched with a learner that the theory will be put into practice. This can be quite a stressful time for them and they should be supported and guided through the process.

The numbers and geographical spread of the participants will dictate how best this support can be provided. If you only have 20 undergraduate mentors all of whom live locally, then a monthly lunchtime meeting will be ideal. In between sessions the coordinator should be available by phone or email to deal with issues of a more urgent nature. You will find that as the mentor support session is brought to their attention by an email, activity between the mentors or coaches and their learners increases. Knowing that they will be asked to report on progress at the impending support workshop encourages them to be more proactive. It is not unusual to observe a flurry of coaching or mentoring activity just prior to a support workshop.

Although this is in itself an advantage, there are many other benefits to holding support workshops, such as improved monitoring of the developing relationships. It will quickly become apparent if there are some common issues emerging. It may be that a large number of your mentors are finding that their mentees are not arriving promptly to the arranged meetings or perhaps not carrying out the actions that have been agreed as part of the sessions. The workshop content can then be arranged around those themes and how to deal with them effectively.

There are some common issues that present themselves as part of many coaching and mentoring schemes. These can be used to plan early support workshop sessions, although the content of future sessions should be arranged accordingly around the emerging issues of your particular programme. For example, you may include, on an academic peer mentoring programme, a session on 'preparing for exams' two months or so prior to exam week. The coaches and mentors can be given further tools and resources that can be used to support revision planning and exam techniques. In the case of re-sits, referrals or deferrals, similarly, further materials and resources can be pertinently provided specifically for this purpose. These tools and activities can be practised on each other within the workshop session to help build confidence in their implementation. For a business mentoring scheme you may include an 'effective CV writing' session if many of the mentees have requested this type of support.

Some basic common themes for support workshops can be as follows:

Dealing with learners who appear reluctant to arrange a meeting

Despite having a thorough application and induction process it is not uncommon for learners to appear to avoid arranging a meeting or fail to respond to an initial email from their coach or mentor. Some will find it difficult to tie down their learner to arrange a meeting or even obtain a response to an email or telephone message. This can unsurprisingly leave them feeling rejected and deflated. It can be extremely demoralising for the eager coach or mentor, and they can often take this seeming rejection very personally. For those who are less confident, it can also deter them from being more persistent in making contact with both their learner and the coordinator.

Having discussed this potential issue at the training and perhaps having it as a 'common issue case study' they will hopefully be prepared for this scenario. However when the situation does actually arise, many can feel that they are in some way to blame and many will assume that they are the only ones to whom it has happened. Holding one of the early support workshops on this topic will help those who have managed to forge a relationship to share their experiences with those who have not. It may be upon reflection that the initial email that the coach or mentor sent was not of a friendly enough nature. Perhaps the tone was too formal.

What the mentors and coaches will find most useful and comforting is hearing that others have similar concerns and that they are not alone. This apparent lack of enthusiasm from their learners often stems from a feeling of being overwhelmed with work or study which very often would have been their reason for applying for support in the first place. It can also be a simple case of 'cold feet' whereby having applied for help they become a little daunted by the thought of embarking upon a relationship with someone who is essentially a complete stranger. If non-response from learners has been identified as an issue, they should be reassured that this is very often normal and in no way a reflection on them personally.

The 'three-strike rule' has been proven to be extremely effective in these cases. This entails the mentor or coach sending an introductory email, telephoning, or sending a text message upon being matched. If there is no response to this then they should send a second message within no more than three days asking if the mentee/coachee has received the first message. At this stage they should also check with the scheme coordinator that they have been given the correct contact details. If no response is received from the second message, the coach or mentor should then send a third and final message, again within three days. This final message should inform the learner that the mentor/coach will be contacting the scheme coordinator to check that they have the correct contact details. They should also state that they will assume from the absence of a reply that they no longer wish to be a part of the programme and that they will be asking the coordinator to match them with another learner. In many cases simply following this procedure will prompt a response from the learner.

This first support workshop can be used to remind mentors and coaches of the 'three-strike rule' and ensure that they are following the procedure correctly. With luck some of the participants will be able to share their experiences of implementing this procedure successfully and some time can be spent drafting possible example emails that relay the message firmly but in a friendly manner.

Managing learners who do not carry out the actions that have been agreed as part of the coaching or mentoring sessions

Many mentors and coaches may have regular meetings and communication with their learner who appears to be engaged with the process. However, whilst good rapport may have been built, if a learner does not commit and carry out the agreed actions, then little progress will be made.

Within the workshop your mentors and coaches should be reminded of the training session on action planning and the need for SMART targets. They should reflect on whether they possibly have too high expectations of their learner or perhaps are not being sufficiently challenging. Some will be reluctant to be more challenging with their learner, but this practice should be encouraged. It can be easy to reach a plateau within a mentoring or coaching relationship, and meeting regularly with their learners is not necessarily a sign of progress. The sessions might comprise of little more than a 'catch-up' and friendly chat. They should be reminded to always agree on a clear action plan and targets for their learners. This can alter the nature of the meetings into 'mentoring' that promotes advancement rather than mere companionship.

You could use the workshop to identify the specific tasks that they have been discussing with their learner and explore in groups how they might be SMARTer. If you have been collecting the contact records regularly, then you will be able to monitor the appropriateness of the targets that have been set.

Mentors and coaches should also be encouraged to ask more challenging questions of their learners to better establish areas for improvement. In pairs they could be instructed to ask each other 'open and challenging' questions about their progress so far and give each other feedback.

Maintaining momentum in the relationship

Some of your mentors and coaches may find that although they have a regular pattern of meetings, the relationship becomes stale. It might seem as though they are meeting more out of habit than usefulness. A number of your mentors and coaches may feel that they are not having an impact on their learner or that they are ineffective.

If this appears to be an issue a good workshop would be for the mentors or coaches to spend time reflecting on the initial goals that their learner wanted to achieve and to assess how close they are to reaching them and what steps have already been made. They may have to be encouraged to look for evidence that some goals have already been reached.

The fact that their learner regularly attends the sessions is usually a sign that they are finding the intervention useful. Most learners will not continue to attend sessions that they feel are not helping. Mentors and coaches are often quite self-critical, and it may help if they work in pairs to encourage each other. Very often they may need to be reminded about the first stage of their mentoring or coaching relationship where they were perhaps finding it difficult to build rapport with their learner. If they are now meeting regularly and are able to talk freely, then this in itself could be construed as progress.

The main points to cover in this workshop would be to ensure that the mentors or coaches ask the learners directly for feedback. Rather than simply ask if the sessions are useful, they should ask questions such as 'What particular aspects of the mentoring are helpful?' or 'Are there things that we do not cover that you would like to?' or 'What aspects of the sessions are least helpful?'

Things to review might be the length of the sessions. It may be that a one-hour session is no longer required and 30–40 minutes would suffice. It may be that they have not as yet utilised any of the coaching and mentoring tools. If not, then it could be suggested that these could be introduced to refresh or invigorate the sessions. Another consideration could be the actions and targets that are set in the sessions. Are these challenging enough or could they be increased? It may be that nothing needs to be done at all and that good progress continues to be made without making any changes.

Prior to this session it may be worth asking the learners for some mid-scheme feedback. This feedback would of course be presented to the mentors and coaches anonymously and so no one person or relationship is identified. The information gleaned from the learners replies could be used to guide the workshop if some common themes are identified.

Managing the end of the relationship

Towards the end of your mentoring programme a workshop should be dedicated to bringing the relationship to a close. Ending a mentoring or coaching relationship is a part of the process that is often overlooked. It is common for the relationship to fade away and the mentor or coach to simply lose contact with their learner without formally bringing it to an end. This period of time should also be an opportunity to reflect upon and review the learning and development that has taken place, not only for their learner but for them too.

Your mentors and coaches should be reminded about the importance of formally ending the relationship, ensuring that their learner does not feel abandoned and exploring the different options available to them. Will they keep in touch from time to time just to check how things are going? Will they continue to meet but as friends rather than mentor and mentee or coach and coachee? Does the relationship need to be extended if the learner has not had sufficient time to achieve his or her goals? These are all possible options within the remit of a mentoring or coaching programme and agreement will need to be reached with all parties involved. Either way these discussions should happen prior to the relationship ending, so the learner is fully prepared for a life without the support of a mentor or coach.

At this particular workshop your participants should explore the possible options available to them and be guided by you on the remit of your particular programme. If they are final-year undergraduates, then they are unlikely to continue participating in your scheme (except as alumni perhaps) or they may have the capacity to continue supporting the same or even another learner.

The final workshop

The very last workshop should be used as a forum to collect feedback that can be used in your evaluation. This could consist of a questionnaire or a focus group, depending on the size of your programme. It should also serve as a thank you for their participation, and if funding allows it will be appreciated if they are treated to refreshments or a buffet lunch etc. If you treat your mentors and coaches well, showing them that they are appreciated, then they will be more likely to volunteer again in the following cycle. They are always very keen to hear feedback from the learners too, which can be given at this stage although the identities of the individual learners should always remain undisclosed. This can be an important aspect, as many of the learners will not show their appreciation directly to their mentor or coach, and so they may feel that their efforts were not appreciated. It is common for mentors and coaches to be uncertain of the impact and progress that they have made with their learners. Hearing positive feedback, albeit perhaps collective and anonymised, will go some way to reassure them that their efforts were not in vain.

If you have a substantial number of mentors or coaches, you may have to deliver a number of themed workshops on a more regular basis and at various times/days of the week to ensure that all the mentors and coaches are able to attend. If using mentors or coaches from the business community or alumni, then evening sessions may be more practical.

Whilst it is a good idea to have planned activities and themes for discussion, this should not monopolise the entire session. An hour to 45 minutes is usually adequate to cover the planned themes and a further 30–40 minutes can be utilised with individual issues that the mentors or coaches wish to discuss.

To involve the whole group with the individual issue of one participant, they can be split into groups and asked to suggest some ideas for solutions which are then fed back to the group as a whole. This approach often works better than merely telling them what they should do. The individual concerned can then select which of the approaches she or he feels will work best with their learner.

Another approach that can be useful, particularly if you have a small group, is for the individual mentor or coach to describe the issue to the rest of the group. When he or she has finished, each member of the group in turn asks the coach or mentor a question to explore the issue further and find a solution. The coach or mentor does not answer any of the questions immediately until each member of the group has asked a question. Instead they decide which of the questions they would like to answer, and the discussion then proceeds with the guidance of the coordinator. From the line of questioning, a resolution for the coach or mentor to try will then hopefully emerge.

Obviously in these workshops, the anonymity of the learners being discussed is essential and the participants should either refer to 'my mentee' or use a pseudonym.

It can be useful to end the session a few minutes early leaving some time for individual coaches or mentors to see you on an individual basis. Some will prefer not to discuss their individual issues in a group session and will appreciate some individual attention.

These workshops should not need to run for more than two hours and in some cases just an hour will suffice. There is little point in keeping participants there when there is little content of interest to be discussed.

▶ Coach or Mentor Forums

Many of the mentoring software packages have a forum facility for both the mentors and the mentees. These can form the basis for mentors and coaches to share their experiences. However they need to be strictly monitored by the mentoring coordinator who can help guide the discussions. The mentors' forum is not generally accessed by the mentees or vice versa.

If you are not utilising a software package that has this facility, a forum can be fairly easily created using closed social media networks such as Facebook or through a university study group. Your mentors and coaches should be directed to this regularly and alerted to the different themes being discussed. They should of course also be encouraged to participate and input into the discussion.

In my experience, classroom-based sessions usually hold the most value as regards learning, but in cases where there is a wide geographical spread of mentors or coaches, then an online forum is probably the most practical way of offering support.

It cannot be stressed too much that having a coordinator available to support mentors/coaches when they are experiencing difficulties in a relationship is essential. Your part of the bargain for the participation of the coaches and mentors should be the promise that you will always respond to a query in 24–48 hours, whether that is by phone or email.

10 Monitoring and Evaluation

It will be important to collect data to demonstrate the impact of your programme for a number of reasons. Not only will you want to know if the programme is effective in achieving its aims, you will also want to know what could be done to improve it. This information is important not only for your own use and to improve practice but may be imperative in order to obtain continued funding.

Evaluation should not be something that is given attention only at the end of the programme; it should be planned right from the implementation. This is why it is so important to establish the aims and objectives of your programme before you begin, as this will guide your evaluation tools and methods.

There is continuing pressure to demonstrate efficacy of these types of intervention in quantitative rather than qualitative terms, particularly if using government funding. Funding organisations are not so impressed these days with large volumes of qualitative and anecdotal evidence from the participants expressing how much they enjoyed the mentoring or how they liked meeting with their coach. They are usually more impressed with data that show impact, such as achieving higher grades, improved student satisfaction scores, or reduced attrition. Whilst this type of data is more difficult to attain, it is not impossible if you collect data pre and post the mentoring or coaching programme.

If for example you wish to demonstrate improved student satisfaction as one of your aims and objectives, you might ask your learners, pre-intervention, how they would rate their satisfaction with student life using a Likert scale. Post-intervention you would then repeat the question and, comparing the given scores from pre- to post-intervention, you will be able to see if there has been any improvement. The greater the participant numbers, the more statistically significant and robust your findings will be. Evidence such as this would not be conclusive however, as there may have been other factors that had improved the student satisfaction scores including the passage of time. The evidence would certainly have more significance if there were a control group of students used for comparison. The control group would consist of a similar category of students who did not participate in the mentoring or coaching. They should have answered the same question at the same time as the mentored or coached group but not have shown the same increase in student satisfaction scores pre to post data collection. Evidence such as this would certainly be more robust, especially if it were presented alongside qualitative data from the participants that corresponded with these findings. The undergraduate peer-coaching case study below shows this type of evaluation method demonstrating improved grades.

CASE STUDY 6
Peer Coaching Programme (UK)

Name of institution: SE University

Name of programme: Peer Coaching

Number of years that the programme has been delivered: Since 2012

Number of coaches: 70 in 2014

Number of coachees:
2012 – 60 (pilot scheme)
2013 – 124
2014 – 165

Who is supported:
Any students who self-refer or those who are signposted by a tutor who recognises that a student is underperforming academically or in danger of failing.

How the need was identified:
Although peer mentoring was already offered within the institution, it was targeted at students from lower socioeconomic groups with the aim of aiding retention and improving social integration. Several requests for mentoring had been received from students who were not from lower socioeconomic groups, specifically requesting academic support with the intention of improving their academic performance. Of those applying for the mentoring programme, many were mainly interested in having a mentor from a similar programme of study. It became apparent that there was a need for a programme of this type specifically to support students with academic attainment. For the pilot scheme it was offered as academic peer mentoring. As the programme focussed specifically on academic attainment, it was offered for a much shorter duration than the peer mentoring, for the avoidance of confusion the decision was taken to rename it 'peer coaching'.

The aims/objectives for the coaching:
The objective for the programme is to improve academic attainment. Whilst the coaches are instructed not to do the work for the coachees or share their own work from previous years, they can guide the coachees on aspects such as essay structure or referencing and with organising their time.

The definition/model of coaching that was adopted:
The face-to-face sessions are mostly conducted on a one-to-one basis and the support is not directive, avoiding 'advice-giving'. Support is also offered through emails and/or Skype/telephone. Email support is conducted through software that monitors the frequency of the contact between coach and coachee and allows the coordinator access, ensuring quality control of the support offered.

How suitable coaches are selected and recruited:
Undergraduates are invited to apply for the role of coach through short recruitment talks given at lectures or induction sessions. Coaches are selected via a process of application form and interview. Two interviewers score each participant with a minimum requirement to be accepted into the programme. Attributes sought include good listening skills and an empathetic attitude as well as a good understanding of the issues faced. Coaches are also required to be performing well academically, at least in their second year at university and on track to achieve a 2:1 or above.

The duration of the coaching relationships:
Ten weeks commencing in December/January.

The coach training plan:
There is a two-day training programme delivered by the mentoring and coaching team. It includes exploring the role of a coach/mentor, communications skills, action planning/target setting, and the application of coaching tools designed specifically to improve academic performance. There is a short assessment that asks the students to respond to a case study scenario and suggest how they might deal with it. It is assessed by the mentoring and coaching team using set criteria to judge their questioning skills, action planning/goal setting, and appropriate use of coaching tools. Successful completion of this assessment is essential for inclusion in the programme.

The coachee induction process:
The programme is promoted through the intranet and student support services and by tutors, although many students have heard of the service by word of mouth. Every student who wishes to apply for a coach is required to complete an application form stating what support he or she requires and to attend either a group or individual induction session. The induction informs them of their responsibilities and of the boundaries of the coaching relationship. They are also allowed to peruse the profiles of the coaches and select the one that they would prefer to work with.

Matching criteria and process:
The pre questionnaires from both the coach and the coachees are used to make best matches where possible, but the choice is also dictated by coach availability. The students' preferred choices from the induction session are also a strong pointer as to whom they are subsequently matched with.

Frequency of the meetings:
A guideline of one meeting per week for an hour's duration is used although many communicate regularly via text and Skype as well.

How the coaches are supported:
The coaches are required as part of their commitment to attend support workshops at least once per month. These are a forum in which to meet fellow coaches and discuss ideas and experiences. They are offered fortnightly throughout the programme. In addition to this an allocated coordinator is available by phone or email to offer advice and support for issues that are of a more urgent nature. Additional training is also offered as part of the workshops on specific common issues such as exam preparation and revision or additional coaching tools or techniques.

The coordinator role:
The programme has an assigned coordinator who works on an equivalent 0.6 FTE basis. However the hours fluctuate from a full-time post at the beginning of the programme to become less intensive once the matching process is completed. The hours are extended again at the end of the programme when the evaluation and data collection take place.

Funding arrangements:
The programme is funded by the individual academic schools that each contribute. In the first year just two academic schools contributed with seven of the schools contributing 2013/14. Due to economies of scale, the cost per academic school was reduced each year.

Evaluation arrangements:
Evaluation is conducted through pre and post questionnaires. A series of questions is asked to establish academic self-efficacy using a Likert scale so that progress can be measured. In the post questionnaire, coachees are also asked to identify the most useful and least useful aspects of the coaching. Using this method it was demonstrated that students' satisfaction levels increased from pre to post coaching as well as motivation/intention to complete their studies. Participants are also given the opportunity to provide qualitative feedback and suggestions for improvement. Feedback is also sought from the coaches and tutors. The evaluation

reports are shared with the academic schools. In 2014 a control group of non-coached students was utilised for comparison with the group who received the peer coaching. The module grade data demonstrated a statistically significant improvement in the grades of the students who received coaching compared to the control group who received no coaching.

Major obstacles in setting up the programme:
Initially coachee referrals and applications were relatively low. However, as the programme was repeated the numbers of applications grew, and in 2014 demand superseded the number of available coaches. Funding initially was difficult to obtain and in the pilot year the programme was supported by just two academic schools.

How these are overcome:
In some areas where there were unmatched coaches but no suitable pending applications, course tutors allowed the coordinator a ten-minute slot within an appropriate lecture to give a short presentation informing students about the service. When a ten-minute slot was not available, the coordinator approached students directly with a leaflet and blank application forms at the end or the beginning of an appropriate lecture as the students were leaving or arriving. This was extremely effective in utilising the coaches who had trained but had not as yet been matched.

After the evaluation had demonstrated improved student satisfaction from pre to post coaching and evidence of retaining students who might have failed or left the university prematurely, the programme was actively funded by the majority of the academic schools in later years.

Programme recommendations:
To combat over-subscription of applications, peer coaches could be trained to deliver small group sessions to complement the individual peer coaching.

As the programme is funded by the individual academic schools, students from the non-participating schools are not offered the opportunity to benefit. It is recommended that a programme such as this is centrally funded so as to serve the whole student population.

You may be able to utilise existing data in your evaluation, taking away the need for a control group. Should you wish to demonstrate reduced attrition rates, you could compare the attrition rate of your coached or mentored group with the average figures held by your institution for a particular course. Similarly this could be achieved by analysing and comparing average grades with those of your mentored or coached group.

There are several reliable questionnaires available to test the academic self-efficacy of students as well as confidence levels and self-esteem. Rather than reinvent questions it may be prudent to utilise these, pre- and post-intervention. However some are quite lengthy and may perhaps be rather off-putting for learners to complete not just once but twice. Your decision will also depend on practicalities such as how easy it will be to obtain them and whether they can be completed electronically or as a paper-based exercise. Questionnaires worth investigating include Richardson's Approaches to Study (1990), Sander and Sanders' Academic Behaviour Confidence scale (2006), and Rosenberg's Measure of Self-Esteem (1965). All consist of Likert scale questions making statistical analysis relatively easy.

Should one of your aims be to assist final-year students to obtain employment or employability skills, this could be measured by asking upon application how satisfied they are with their CV or how confident they are about finding employment after graduation. They could be asked how many applications for employment they have made so far or how prepared they feel for the world of work, using a Likert scale. They could be asked about their career choice and whether they have as yet made a decision about which path to follow. Other questions to follow this could be around their knowledge of their selected career, for example:

How much knowledge do you have about your chosen career path?

No knowledge at all   A great deal of knowledge

1	2	3	4	5	6	7

These questions could all be repeated post-intervention so that comparisons can be made. Of course the questions are all quite subjective but trends may be seen if the number of participants is large enough.

When collecting feedback from learners it would be advisable to assure them that the information that they give you will not be passed on to their coach or mentor. They should always be reassured that the information will be de-identified in any reports etc. and that their honest views and opinions are appreciated.

It can be fruitful to collect mid-scheme feedback from the learners in order that changes deemed necessary might be made sooner rather than later. If you have a rolling programme whereby matching takes place over a long period, you may receive feedback from learners who have been matched for some time, informing you that they found the induction session difficult to attend as there was too little choice in times and/or dates. They might inform you that they would have preferred a different mentor or coach or perhaps more choice in the process. These are adjustments that could be fairly quickly incorporated by increasing the number of induction sessions available or allowing more involvement in the matching process. These changes could benefit the learners who are still applying.

It may be that the mid-way feedback identifies a need for more help with a specific topic such as exam revision. If this were the case, then a forthcoming support workshop could be used to give the coaches or mentors further guidance on how to support in this area.

Whilst quantitative data can be very valuable, some information is better gleaned using a qualitative approach. These questions should be open and can help you to determine which particular aspects of the programme were useful and which were not.

Examples of questions that could be used post intervention include:

▶ Which aspect/s of the mentoring was/were most useful?
▶ Which aspect/s of the coaching was/were least useful?
▶ In what way/s?
▶ What recommendations would you make to improve the service?
▶ Would you recommend the programme to other students? If so, why/ why not?

Using online platforms such as Survey Monkey to collect data might be more appropriate for participants who have a wide geographical spread. One drawback of collecting data via this method is that it can come back anonymously, which limits its use. For example, if the data collected are anonymous, you may not be able to see any trends forming such as the intervention being more or less useful for one particular type of student.

It may be that final-year students find a coaching intervention less useful than those in their first year or those studying Law find it less helpful than those studying Psychology. If using an online platform you will need to consider whether you are likely to require more detailed information such as year of study, course, etc. Of course if you are collecting post-intervention data that are not anonymous you will be able to match the details of each participant with their original application/profile form which will contain all this useful data.

Focus groups can be very useful in obtaining more detailed information about the service. You could offer, funding allowing, a voucher to participants for attendance at a focus group to encourage attendance. The questions asked need not be different from the paper-based questionnaire, but you will be able to prompt attendees for further details. It should not need to be emphasised that the prompts should not be leading, and both negative and positive comments should be followed up. If attendees state that their coach was very helpful you can ask 'In what way?' Should they announce that they got better grades as a result of the mentoring you can ask 'How do you know that?'

It is worth bearing in mind that sometimes peer pressure in focus groups can affect the findings. If one member of the focus group has particularly strong opinions, this can sometimes result in others with less confidence agreeing with that person's comments. It will be important to ensure that all members of the group are allowed to input into the discussions.

Other methods for encouraging participant feedback could be to offer a voucher for the first ten feedback forms received or to offer a prize draw once all the questionnaires are received. Persistence will often pay and a series of email reminders requesting that they send back the questionnaire will not go amiss. If you are particularly low on feedback questionnaires, then it may be prudent to telephone the participants and conduct a 'telephone interview'. You can simply ask them the questions on your questionnaire and note down their replies verbatim. If you can obtain at least a 50 per cent response rate then, depending on total numbers, your findings should be representative of the programme as a whole.

If you are collecting feedback from younger participants, perhaps school pupils, then use of an 'interactive voting system' will make the process a little more enjoyable than completing a paper-based form. Obviously there are costs involved in the purchase of such systems, but they may be available anyway within your institution and can be utilised in your evaluation. Data collection is then conducted through a presentation. A question is displayed on the screen and the participants register their answer through an individually held handset. The handsets can be programmed so that individual participants can be recognised or the data can be recorded collectively. If using this method the question types will be restricted and it does not allow qualitative data to be given. It will be restricted to questions such as:

How useful did you find the mentoring in helping you select a higher education course?

▶ A = no use at all
▶ B = slightly useful
▶ C = useful
▶ D = very useful

The advantage of this method is that the data are recorded immediately onto a PC and can be presented as graphs, pie charts, etc. for inclusion in your report. Younger participants will also enjoy the anonymity that this method brings and the fact that they are using technology. They also enjoy seeing the collective results of the questions being displayed immediately after they have answered each question.

Often a variety of data collection methods is best, particularly a mix of quantitative and qualitative data. The usual guidelines should be implemented when analysing the data to ensure that negative comments are not disregarded. Where there are negative comments, further exploration may show possible reasons. For example, it may be that you have just two or three negative comments about the coaching being unhelpful in a total of 50 responses. Further investigation may show that the negative responses all came from participants who had been allocated the same coach. This information may shed more light on the quality or robustness of your mentor selection process rather than indicating that the coaching intervention was unhelpful.

Mentoring and coaching are, of course, complex interventions and other factors will also need to be taken into account such as frequency of meetings and communication. In the example above, it may be found that the three negative responses were all received from participants who only had one meeting with their coach. The other participants may all have had ten or more coaching sessions. These results will enable you to explore how to improve your programme. It may be that a more rigorous coordinator prompting regime is required to ensure contact is maintained between coach and learner or perhaps a more stringent induction process to ensure that learners are fully engaged.

It may not be until the programme has been repeated two or three times that a final formula is found to obtain optimum results. Of course participants may also suggest improvements that are impractical. They may suggest that the mentoring is extended into a second year when the mentors are final-year students who will have left the institution by then. However, no suggestions should be automatically dismissed without any consideration, particularly if they are mentioned more than once.

▶ Coach and Mentor Feedback

Whilst the learners are likely to be the main focus of your evaluation, the mentors and coaches themselves should not be excluded from the evaluation process. This should start on completion of the training programme. It is essential that they are asked if the training met their expectations and if they felt that it prepared them for the role. Of course this is based purely on perception as they will not actually know this for certain until they start working with a learner. It will however give you an indication as to whether they feel confident about embarking on a mentoring or coaching relationship. They could be asked what else they would like included or which aspects of the training were least and most helpful.

It is good practice to ask them again, one they have embarked on a coaching or mentoring relationship, how well the training prepared them for the role. Having experienced a coaching or mentoring relationship, they should have a better idea of what would have been useful to include in or exclude from the training programme.

It is always useful to ask the mentors and coaches their views on how the relationship has impacted on their learner and also how this manifested itself. This can be compared to the data collected from the learners to check for any correlation. It would not be unusual for mentors or coaches to report increased confidence in their learners, but it is important for them to be able to state exactly how this increased confidence manifested itself. Focus groups can also be very useful for this type of data collection.

The support workshops can be an extremely useful venue for mentor or coach feedback and could be incorporated into the session from time to time. This continuous feedback will be invaluable for you to monitor the progress and identify any issues. If a particular concern has been raised within the support workshops, then it would be prudent to include some specific questions on this in the final evaluation questionnaire so that it can be explored more thoroughly. Focus groups for mentors and coaches can also provide rich data to enhance your final report.

It is wise to also collect data on the impact that coaches'/mentors' participation has had for them. The literature suggests that being a coach or mentor can have a significant impact on a person's skills. This can range from improved confidence to achieving better grades. Whilst your programme may not be targeting them specifically, these hidden benefits can be useful in persuading funding providers to continue supporting the intervention. This sort of evidence can also be extremely useful when recruiting and attracting new mentors or coaches.

It may be possible to collect data from third parties such as tutors who may have observed some changes in the actions and behaviours of the learners. Whilst this will be mainly anecdotal, when presented alongside the learner plus the coach or mentor findings it can present a powerful case to demonstrate impact.

▶ **The Final Report**

A scheme report can be as lengthy or minimal as you wish and the content will depend almost entirely on the demands of your stakeholders. A rough guide for the layout would be:

Executive Summary
This is only required if your final report is very lengthy. It should summarise on one sheet of A4 the background, process, and main findings of your mentoring or coaching programme.

Introduction/Background

▶ highlight the need for support
▶ set the context for the report
▶ give details of the funding arrangements
▶ specify the aims and objectives of the programme
▶ justify the case for a coaching or mentoring intervention
▶ give a brief explanation of who took part and duration/timing
▶ specify target outputs/anticipated impact

Process
This should detail the format for the programme and include the following:

▶ specify number of participants (including those who dropped out)
▶ recruitment criteria and selection of the mentors or coaches
▶ the training programme including participant feedback
▶ learner recruitment criteria and induction process
▶ the matching process
▶ details of the coach or mentor support workshops
▶ the evaluation methods used

Findings

▶ learner feedback
▶ coach or mentor feedback
▶ tutor/staff feedback
▶ your own observations
▶ direct quotes from all participants that substantiate any claims that they have made about benefits/drawbacks
▶ include both negative and positive aspects

Conclusion and Recommendations

Here you should draw attention to the main themes from your data, pointing out the impact that has been achieved. This section should also include any negative impact and highlight any weaknesses in the methodology used to collect the data that may affect the results. For example a very low response rate of feedback questionnaires will be prohibitive in using the data as representative of the whole group.

Any recommendations for the future should also be included in this section as regards the process adopted or perhaps recommending it for a particular type or category of student where it appeared to be more successful.

The final word on evaluation is to not become complacent that your scheme is being delivered in the optimal way. It is essential to keep regularly evaluating the programme as situations and circumstances change, and there may be alternative and improved methods of delivery that could be piloted. Sharing findings with other institutions will also be invaluable in discovering other methods for delivery that may be more effective.

11 Ementoring

Ementoring is an option that many higher education institutions may wish to consider particularly when designing an alumni or business mentoring programme. Whilst greater numbers can be included in the programme, there are certainly as many disadvantages as advantages to this method.

The advantages include:

▶ Closer monitoring of mentoring relationships if using ementoring software
▶ Greater numbers of participants over a wider geographical spread
▶ Low or no cost in travel expenses to be paid
▶ Easier for external mentors to take part as less time consuming
▶ Can fit in more easily if participants have a busy schedule (after working hours)
▶ Can be more cost effective in terms of coordinator hours
▶ Participants have more thinking/response time and are therefore less likely to make mistakes
▶ Written record of communication reduces need for providing contact records
▶ For some learners it will be less intimidating, allowing more freedom in discussions
▶ For young people, safety risk is if using ementoring software

The disadvantages include:

▶ A possible lack of engagement with remote communication
▶ Lacks immediacy and flow of dialogue
▶ Mentor training can be less effective when delivered online
▶ Not so appropriate if more emotional issues arise
▶ More difficult for coordinator to build rapport with participants
▶ More difficult for participants to build rapport with each other
▶ Written words can be more easily misinterpreted
▶ Support workshops may be more difficult to arrange
▶ More difficult to monitor relationships if not using ementoring software

Certainly in my experience, it is more difficult for participants to build rapport when communicating via email. However with Skype and other forms of video messaging this barrier can, to some degree, be overcome. It would certainly not be recommended if the anticipated support is likely to include issues of a more emotional or personal nature. For more practical aims and objectives, such as career mentoring, it can certainly be a useful medium. The discussions in this type of programme are more likely to be functional and better suited to email exchanges.

If it is feasible, then a compromise may be found by arranging a networking event whereby the mentors can have a face-to-face meeting with their mentees. This can help cement the relationship, and email exchanges following the initial meeting may work very well. If there is no opportunity at all for a face-to-face meeting, then the participants will need to work harder at building rapport.

The training programme for the mentors will consist of the same topics, but it will be necessary to include a session on email communication and how this can require more consideration than face-to-face communication. Some dos and don'ts that will need to be conveyed to the participants include:

Dos

▶ Before replying to an email, ensure that it has been read then re-read fully and that it has not just been given a cursory glance
▶ Use bullet points if asking a number of different questions
▶ Respond to emails promptly, sticking to agreed timescales, or send a one-liner explaining the delay, stating when you will come back to them with a full response
▶ Using your learner/coachee/mentee's first name in each message is more friendly
▶ Use proper English with punctuation, grammar, and capital letters, even if the learner does not
▶ Quote back small parts or phrases from their email when replying to them to clarify your answer, as this creates more conversational flow
▶ Be clear and precise at all times, as there are no clues to pick up on such as tone of voice
▶ Always sign off your message personally
▶ Remember that humour, particularly sarcasm, does not translate well in written form – what is intended as jest may just be perceived as rudeness
▶ Always re-read your message before sending to check for anything that may be misconstrued

Don'ts

▶ Don't persistently use capital letters
▶ Avoid using tabs and similar keys as they can be realigned when read on another PC

▶ Don't ask too many questions in one email, three to four at most
▶ Always remember that your learner may have very different opinions and feelings from yours – so beware of offering your opinions too freely
▶ Avoid using text language and over-use of emoticons

In addition to this and if appropriate to your programme, it would be advisable to spend time on the training to guide the mentors in writing their first email. Obviously this will depend on whether you are putting the onus on your mentors or your mentees to make the first contact. If it will be the responsibility of the mentor then it is imperative that the tone of this first email is set appropriately. It should be professional and yet friendly.

The best method to convey this message can be to show poor examples of a first email, allowing the participants to identify what is wrong. An example of a poor introductory email can be found in Box 11.1.

Box 11.1 First example of a poor introductory email

Hi Jamil

I have been allocated to you as your mentor to help support you with any issues that you may be having at the university. I am in my final year here and studying Accounting & Finance. So far things have gone really well for me, but I have worked hard and put a lot of time and effort into my studies so I feel that I will deserve the first class degree that I am heading for. My plan is to work for a large firm of accountants and become Head of Finance for a large international organisation so that I can fulfil my dream to travel.

I selected the course as my father is also in Financial Management and has been very successful in his career. I knew from a young age that this was the path that I wanted to follow and I was always good at Maths.

Let me know if there is anything else that you want to know about me, and I will do my best to help you achieve your potential when we work together.

Hope to hear from you soon

Mohammed

The example in Box 11.1 focuses too much attention on the mentor who shows little interest in the mentee. The example in Box 11.2 is another example of a poor email.

Box 11.2 Second example of a poor introductory email

Hello Amber

I understand that we have been allocated to work together on the mentoring scheme. If I am to support you it will help me if I know the following details:

1. *What final modules you selected as part of your course?*
2. *What grades/marks you have achieved so far?*
3. *What employability skills you want me to help you to develop?*
4. *How exactly you would like me to support you?*
5. *What time/date you would like to meet?*

I would also like you to send me a copy of your CV so that I can start looking at how we can improve it. Once I hear from you with the answers to the above, we can get started.

All the best

Carole

Whilst it would be useful to have the answers to all of the questions posed in the example email in Box 11.2, the tone is generally quite unfriendly.

The third example email in Box 11.3 could be considered a good approach, although each mentor will have their own style which should be allowed to emerge. Importantly the email closes with suggestions of dates to meet that should prompt a response. The example in Box 11.3 can be used as a guide although mentors should be encouraged to use their own terminology.

Box 11.3 Example of a good introductory email

Hello Sabina

I understand that I have been selected to work with you on the Mentoring scheme, so I just wanted to introduce myself.

I am in my third year at TransGlobal Enterprises as an Accountant and have really enjoyed it, although it has not always been a smooth path! I selected Accounting and Global Finance as my final optional modules when I was studying at SE University in 2013, which I think were instrumental in my getting this job. I would be interested to know your final module choices. Perhaps we have some in common?

I have managed to combine my MA studies with work quite successfully so far and understand that you are considering postgraduate studies too. I can't promise to know the answers to all your questions but what I don't know I will attempt to find out.

My work schedule is reasonably flexible at the moment and I am available Mon to Weds in the late afternoon or I am often on campus on Thursdays for my MA course. Let me know which of those days/times suits you best.

As you make the decision to either apply for employment or further study, I will do my best to assist you with that choice.

I'm looking forward to hearing more about you when we meet.

All the best

Justine

Even if you are adopting an ementoring approach entirely rather than a face-to-face programme, it is still necessary to thoroughly train the mentors. An online mode for training should be made available, and mentors should only be matched once they have completed this successfully. Merely sending mentors a pack to read, no matter how comprehensive this might be, does not guarantee that they have read and understood it. Mentors need to demonstrate their commitment to the programme by undertaking the training in the same way as classroom-based training.

The case study below shows how webinars are used to train alumni mentors who cannot attend face-to-face sessions.

CASE STUDY 7
Career Mentoring Programme (Alumni) (Australia)

Name of institution: University of Tasmania

Name of programme: Career Mentor Programme

Number of years that the programme has been delivered: Since 2011

Number of mentors:
2012 with 20 alumni mentors
2014 with 182 registered mentors and 94 matched to student mentees

Number of mentees: 2014 – 126

Who is supported:

University of Tasmania students who have completed at least 12 months of their degree are invited to participate, from undergraduate through to postgraduate programmes. The programme is open to domestic or international enrolments, full-time and part-time, and both on-campus and distance students. However, participation is dependent on the availability of a suitable mentor, which is explained to the students on application.

How the need was identified:

A Student Services and Amenities Fees survey indicated that 'Career Support' was in the top five areas of interest, indicating that this kind of programme would be of benefit to the students.

The aims/objectives for the mentoring:

The aims of the programme are to
- assist the mentee to build information about career direction
- provide the mentee with an opportunity to increase confidence and familiarity with aspects of workplace culture
- assist mentors to enhance leadership and interpersonal communication skills
- assist mentors to keep up to date with current knowledge within their field through contact with current university students
- develop mutually beneficial relationships between the university, its students, and its alumni

The definition/model of mentoring that was adopted:

The definition given to our mentors and mentees is from Eric Parsloe, the Oxford School of Coaching and Mentoring:

'Mentoring is to support and encourage people to manage their own learning in order that they may maximise their potential, develop their skills, improve their performance and become the person they want to be.'

The majority of the relationships are one to one with a handful of small-group mentoring sessions. Suggestions for support areas are provided, but the mentor/mentee agree on what themes are best for them. Communication is by face to face, email, telephone, and Skype.

How suitable mentors are selected and recruited:

Mentors are almost entirely University of Tasmania alumni with at least two years' professional experience. This gives mentors an additional connection with the students, having shared similar undergraduate or postgraduate student experiences.

Advertisements for mentors are carried out through Alumni Relations, as well as recruiting through the University of Tasmania's own networks when an alumni mentor cannot be identified.

The duration of the mentoring relationships:
Mentors and mentees attend information sessions in March. Matching is completed by the end of April, and an official programme launch is held in late April. Limited matching may occur after this time, depending on availability of mentors. The formal programme runs for six months. In addition, some relationships continue on an informal basis beyond the official close.

For further support an on campus launch, a mid-year networking session, and end-of-year celebration events are also provided.

The mentor training plan:
New programme mentors attend a briefing session prior to being matched with a student. This provides an overview of the programme, discussion of suggested themes and activities that might be covered through the mentoring relationship, and a set of roles and responsibilities of both mentors and mentees.

Distance mentors (based outside Tasmania) are invited to a pre-programme webinar that covers similar concepts to the new mentor face-to-face session. Mentors are provided with a Career Mentor Programme Participant Manual including a Mentor Agreement.

The mentee induction process:
Mentees are required to attend an information session prior to registering for the programme. This session introduces the concept of mentoring, outlines the process of matching, and clearly defines roles and responsibilities of mentors and mentees. Mentees are also provided with a Career Mentor Programme Participant Manual and access to a LinkedIn Discussion Group.

At their first meeting, mentors and mentees are required to complete a Mentoring Agreement. This document clarifies the expectations of the mentor and mentee and lists agreed themes for exploration by the pair.

It is made clear to mentees that they are the driving force in the relationship. Mentees are expected to make initial contact, arrange meetings, and determine the focus of the relationship.

Matching criteria and process:
Mentors and mentees are matched manually, based on professional interest and degree background.

Frequency of the meetings:
Participants are required to make contact at least four times throughout the programme. This can be face-to-face, telephone, email, or Skype. Face-to-face meetings might take place at the mentor's workplace, on campus, or in a café.

How the mentors are supported:
Mentors are supported throughout by the Career Mentor Programme Coordinator, who responds to individual requests as they arise. Mentors also have access to a LinkedIn discussion group.

The Mentoring Coordinator role:
For the first two years the programme was supported by a Career Development Counsellor alongside other responsibilities. The availability of Student Services and Amenities Fees (SSAF) funding in 2013 and 2014 allowed for the creation of a full-time Career Mentor Programme Coordinator position. The Programme Coordinator also supports other team members as appropriate.

Funding arrangements:
The Career Mentor Programme was initially a pilot conducted in response to Career Staff research and experiences. For the past two years the programme has been funded through Student Services and Amenities Fees. The student body vote each year on how to spend SSAF funding, and the students have chosen to support the programme. 'Career Education' has been in the top five areas of interest for students at the University of Tasmania.

Evaluation arrangements:
All programme participants are invited to complete a confidential online evaluation. Questions in the evaluation target each of the programme's aims.

Major obstacles in setting up the programme:
- Time and funding for the Career Mentoring Programme Coordinator Role
- Identification of suitable mentors
- An effective matching process takes a long time
- Students losing interest after initial meeting with mentor

How these are overcome:
- Prioritising project and availability of dedicated funding
- Developing strong relationship with Alumni Relations for identifying mentors and assisting with programme events

▶ Continual strengthening of relationships with mentors across four years of programme
▶ Conversations with career practitioners at other institutions – shared experiences from other programmes has improved our approach

Programme Recommendations:
▶ Increasing participation for off-campus students, through intensified recruitment and stronger support
▶ Further clarity for student mentees on the purpose of the programme and, importantly, what it is *not* about
▶ Expand scope of the programme to include focus on the elite athlete programme and indigenous student cohort
▶ Plans to expand the scope of the programme to include ideas such as 'a day in the life', allowing access to mentors who are unable to commit to a full programme

▶ Ementoring Software

There is an increasing number of software packages available to aid ementoring programmes. All have differing facilities that will suit some programmes but not others. Some will allow the coordinator to access the email communication which can be extremely useful in monitoring the developing relationships. Access to the email communication can also allow a coordinator to intervene in the event of any concerns. Some mentors will appreciate the fact that a coordinator can access their communication and give guidance on their mentoring skills if they are uncertain that they are doing a good job. If using software that allows coordinator access, then participants must be informed that this is the case. It should be explained that although emails will not be accessed routinely, the coordinator is able to view the communication but will only do so if there are concerns.

Good software will also include robust reporting facilities that can inform the coordinator when there has been no activity between mentor and mentee for ten days or more. This can be particularly useful to give timely prompts to your mentors or mentees who have been slow to respond to an email.

There may be other facilities available such as being able to blanket email all 'inactive mentors' following a search. This can save a considerable amount of coordinator time and will ensure that the relationships maintain momentum. When your participants are aware that a coordinator is monitoring the frequency and email response time, it usually has the desired effect of making them more responsive.

Other software will enable participants to create a profile and select the mentor or mentee of their choice. The mechanisms for this differ and you will need to carefully select the one that is most suited to your needs. It has to be said that a number of these products are very ineffective or not particularly user friendly. If this is the case your participants are likely to simply exchange personal emails and communicate outside of the system without your knowledge. Should this happen it makes any form of monitoring difficult, if not impossible.

It is worth checking whether participants have to log onto the system in order to communicate with their learner or mentor as this can also be a deterrent to use. Systems that allow the users to utilise their own email address are often preferable. Other systems have the facility to text a participant when an email has been sent to them so that they know to log into the system to access it.

Many of these ementoring systems have a mechanism in place for screening and preventing emails being sent if they contain profanity or inappropriate dialogue which can be useful. These security measures can also be extended to mask telephone numbers, addresses, weblinks or email contacts if they are incorporated into an email or to prevent attachments being sent until they have been approved by a coordinator. These facilities can be extremely useful and indeed essential if you have young people taking part in your programme.

It is not the aim of this text to make any recommendations for particular software, as this would be futile with new products continually becoming available. It is recommended that a thorough exploration is made of what is available within your funding restrictions, as the packages are generally expensive and you are likely to be tied in to at least a one-year contract. Mistakes can be costly, and if you can talk to other institutions that use such a product, then I would suggest that you do so to glean as much information as you can. A reputable supplier should be happy to give you the contact names of existing customers for you to talk to prior to purchase.

It is not essential to purchase ementoring software; you could simply allow your participants to contact each other directly. If your programme is small, then it would not be financially viable to spend this amount of money until the programme has grown in numbers sufficiently. Note though that you will not be able to monitor the relationships as closely without this type of software in place and so you will be entirely reliant on your participants for feedback and to keep you informed of progress.

Mentees too will need a similar induction and application process, even if it is an ementoring programme. In some respects this is even more essential to demonstrate their commitment to the programme. The induction could be conducted online, over the phone or face to face, again depending on your particular programme.

The evaluation process with ementoring should in some respects be easier than with a face-to-face programme as participants will be used to completing online documents. However this does not preclude using other methods such as telephone interviews or focus groups to collect the data.

12 School Mentoring Programmes

As will have been seen from Chapter 5, you will need specific criteria if you wish to recruit mentors to work with school pupils. There are other considerations that need to be taken into account, such as the need for knowledge of the education system and curriculum of the country where the mentoring is taking place. For some schemes this will be an essential criterion, for example if you are supporting secondary school pupils with their academic performance or qualification and exam subject choices. It may be beneficial to recruit students from particular backgrounds such as lower socioeconomic groups, those who have been in the care system or perhaps had behavioural issues when they were younger. Attracting suitable students can be accomplished by mentioning in your promotional materials and talks that applications would be welcome from people with these backgrounds. It is likely that students who share a similar background to their mentee will be able to build a better rapport and empathise more easily than if not. However it is not essential in all cases and it may not be practical to do so in sufficient numbers. A well-trained and well-intentioned mentor too can build a good rapport with a young person even if she or he has not faced such barriers her- or himself. It is worth noting that young people, in particular, often prefer a more pragmatic type of support when facing barriers, as opposed to sympathy. This is why mentoring can be so beneficial for them, as good mentoring follows just this type of approach.

Pupils under the age of five are likely to be unsuitable for a mentoring programme. It would be prudent to only utilise experienced mentors with younger children as working with pupils under the age of ten is generally more challenging and requires greater expertise.

As was seen in Chapter 3, there are a number of aims and objectives that you may wish to achieve through the mentoring programme. Identifying these will, as with an adult mentoring programme, help guide your evaluation process. The difference will be in the way your questions are phrased. Asking too many open and reflective questions is likely to result in non-responses. For young people the total number of questions should be reduced and where possible should merely require a tick box using Likert scale questions. For very young pupils, smiley or sad faces can help maintain their interest in the process. Presenting questions such as the ones below, which were used as part of a mentoring transition programme, can provide valuable data:

Were you worried about moving on to secondary school before seeing your mentor?

Has working with your mentor made you less worried about going to secondary school?

If affordable and available, then an interactive voting system could be used for data collection as discussed on page 125. This allows the data to be collected through individual handsets without the need for paper-based questionnaires. Children usually enjoy this process for giving their opinions rather than finding it a chore.

When working with schools and if the mentors are likely to be visiting the school premises, it is essential to have some form of 'project agreement' in place. This should lay out the responsibilities of both parties. Your undertaking would likely be to adequately prepare and train the mentors, provide support, and induct the mentees. The school's responsibility would consist of allowing children out of lessons to attend the mentoring sessions (if need be) and providing suitable accommodation for the mentoring sessions to take place (such as a meeting room with a window or any room where they will be undisturbed). The school's responsibility should also include a suitable mechanism for alerting pupils to the fact that they have a mentoring session, so that the mentors are not kept waiting for too long. Whilst the agreement will not be a legal document, it will assist the programme to run more smoothly if everyone is aware of their responsibilities.

It is also strongly advised that a child protection policy and guidelines are utilised that give guidance on working with children and vulnerable people. This should inform all your participants of behaviours to adopt and avoid when working with children and should include appropriate use of language as well as appropriate and inappropriate physical contact. There should also be clear guidelines about what to do should a young person indicates that he or she is being abused, is involved in criminal activity, is being harmed or causing harm to others.

▶ **School Mentor Training**

The mentor training would need particular emphasis on confidentiality and duty of disclosure. With adults, any worrying issues would be brought to the attention of the coordinator to deal with. However, in school mentoring programmes the school is likely to have a procedure and dedicated individual in place for reporting such issues. It is essential that this procedure is clearly defined between the school and the higher education institution and conveyed to the mentors. It is worth adding another layer of security around this issue to avoid any confusion later on. It is recommended that the mentors sign a written agreement stating that they have read and understood the child protection guidelines and agree to abide by them. This alerts them to the seriousness of following the correct procedure and will protect you, as the coordinator, should they deviate from these guidelines.

The common issues session, activity 16 of the chapter on mentor training, is likely to need adapting to include the type of issues that might be more common with young people. This could include scenarios such as the following:

Example 1
Sam tells you that she wants to be a veterinary surgeon when she leaves school, but her grades so far are extremely poor and she is unlikely to perform sufficiently well to apply for a place at university.

Example 2
Chloe tells you that she is always in trouble at school and often get detentions but says that it isn't her fault and that the teachers pick on her.

Example 3
Ben is very clever but says that he hates school and intends to leave as soon as he is able so that he can get a job and start earning money. Neither of his parents went to university and they say that studying is a waste of time. They agree that Ben should start working as soon as he can.

▶ **School Mentoring Toolkits**

The tools that are provided for your mentors will also need to be adapted for use with young people. There are a number of easily accessible activities that can be utilised for mentoring such as Tim Pickles (1992) or Salter & Twidle (2010). It is useful to separate mentoring tools into those suitable for older children aged 11+ and those suitable for young children aged 5–11.

Mentoring tools for older pupils should contain activities to develop good study skills, whilst those for younger pupils should include activities around more emotional issues.

The case study below shows an example of how one university provides mentoring to school pupils based on the needs of the individual schools. Small group mentoring is provided where it has been found that the pupils prefer this to the one-to-one sessions.

CASE STUDY 8
School Pupil Mentoring Programme (UK)

Name of institution: SE University

Name of programme: Raising Aspirations

Number of years that the programme has been delivered: Six years

Number of mentors: 30 per year

Number of mentees: Approximately 130 per year

Who is supported: Secondary school pupils – Year 9/10/11 (ages 13–16)

How the need was identified:
Schools in the local area with pupils from lower socioeconomic groups and with low progression to higher education were identified to receive the support using government data. Mentees need to have the potential to achieve five A* to C grades at GCSE and must not have a family tradition of higher education attendance. They may also face other barriers to educational success such as disability, being in care, being a young carer or having English as a second language, etc.

The aims/objectives for the mentoring:
The objectives of the programme are to encourage young people to engage with their education, to motivate them towards success, to consider course choices and career paths, and to raise their aspirations towards higher education. The programme also aims to raise attainment by encouraging pupils to adopt better study habits. Each school selects the pupils whom they wish to take part and agrees the mentoring agenda with the university. This information is recorded on the Project Agreement that is drawn up and signed by the University Coordinator and the Head Teacher from each of the schools.

The definition/model of mentoring that was adopted:
The contact consists of one to one and sometimes includes some small group meetings, face-to-face meetings only, or a mixture of face-to-face sessions with an element of ementoring in between meetings.

The mentoring approach uses solutions-focussed methods and is non-directive. There is no predetermined agenda for the sessions, and the aim is to empower the young people to make their own decisions and take ownership of their education and future prospects.

How suitable mentors are selected and recruited:
Undergraduates are invited to apply for the role of mentor through short recruitment talks given at lectures or induction sessions and through the intranet. Mentors are selected via a process of application forms and short interviews. Two interviewers score each participant with a minimum requirement to be accepted into the programme. Assessment continues during the training programme, and any who are deemed unsuitable for the role are not matched.

The duration of the mentoring relationships:
Ten to twelve weeks commencing in January

The mentor training plan:
A two-day training programme is delivered by the mentoring coordinator and colleagues from the mentoring team. It includes investigating the role of a mentor, communications skills, action planning and target setting, methods and techniques and tools for mentoring.

Every mentor is provided with a mentoring toolkit, split into different sections: Different Learning Styles, Getting to Know Your Mentee, Exploring Attitudes to School, Making Choices & Taking Control, Setting Goals, and Study Skills, plus a section for younger children entitled Exploring the Self. As part of the training mentors practise the tools on each other and apply them to case study scenarios.

There is a short written assessment held at the end of the training to test the trainees' understanding. They are asked to respond to a case study scenario and suggest how they might deal with it. There is a further half-day top-up training session once the mentoring has commenced.

The mentee induction process:
The mentees are initially recommended for the programme by school staff. They are then given a presentation by the mentoring coordinator to explain the aims and objectives of the programme, what to expect from the mentor and how to make best use of the opportunity. At this stage they also have the opportunity to meet some of the mentors. They complete a pre-mentoring questionnaire/profile form to establish what they might like support with. They are given the option to opt out if they so wish.

Matching criteria and process:
The pre-mentoring questionnaire/profile is used to make the best matches with mentors where possible, but mostly matching is dictated by practical

issues such as when mentors are free to go into schools and teachers' knowledge of which pupils would work well together in the event of group work.

Frequency of the meetings:
Once a week in school for 40–60 minutes per meeting. Usually class-room or meeting room space is found so that the sessions can be con-ducted confidentially. If possible, mentees are invited to the university for a half-day at the end of the programme to meet their mentors for the last session. They are given a tour of the campus by their mentor who shows them areas that are of particular interest, such as aircraft simula-tors, the Faculty of Art and Design, and the motor sport engineering department.

How the mentors are supported:
The mentors are undergraduates from the university and receive weekly/fortnightly support from the mentoring coordinator who regu-larly attends the schools where the sessions are taking place. The coord-inator is also available via email or phone throughout the programme delivery.

The Mentoring Coordinator role:
The programme has an assigned coordinator who works on average three days a week on the project.

Funding arrangements:
The programme is funded by the university's Widening Participation budget although it was originally Government funded. For some schools it has been offered on a partly subsidised basis if the referred pupils do not fully fulfil the criteria but are still considered by the school to be in need of additional support.

Evaluation arrangements:
This is conducted through pre and post questionnaires. A series of ques-tions is asked to establish attitudes towards higher education and inten-tion to apply, using a Likert scale so that progress can be measured. In the post questionnaire, mentees are also asked to identify aspects with which their mentor has helped them with a simple Yes, No, Don't Know, or Not Discussed. They are also given the opportunity to provide qualitative feedback. Feedback is also sought from the mentors and the school staff. The evaluation reports are shared with the schools.

Major obstacles in setting up the programme:
Communicating with busy teachers in schools. Finding suitable space for the mentoring to take place. Matching mentors to schools given

complications over availability and travel options, etc. Mentees not being informed of the planned session time or forgetting their appointment time.

How these are overcome:
By being adaptable and by making the programme as easy to run for the schools as possible. Seeking solutions and having sufficient time to trouble shoot on a daily basis.

Programme recommendations:
The programme changes slightly each year according to circumstance, but changes have come about as a result of the evaluation process, for example changing the ratio of group work vs. one to one sessions when it was found that pupils in some schools preferred the group sessions to one to one meetings.

Ensuring that systems are put in place for mentors to report to the coordinator in a way that can be shared with schools and not break confidentiality.

If your programme will include some email contact then it will be essential to purchase an ementoring licence to enable this to happen securely. Ensure that the platform that you purchase has all the required facilities, such as screening for profanity, blocking attachments, and blocking messages that contain telephone numbers, addresses, or email contacts. However you will find in the case of young pupils that face-to-face mentoring is more likely to be effective. As with adults, a combination of face-to-face and ementoring can work best. One advantage to ementoring with children is that many of the ementoring licences and platforms designed for young people allow access as part of the provision to useful materials such as university course entry requirements, study/revision skills resources and career information. These can be extremely useful for the mentors, though creating your own resources will enable you to provide more personalised materials to better suit the context of your specific mentoring programme. A thorough investigation of the resources offered will be necessary to ensure that they suit the requirements and are age appropriate for your programme. Chapter 11 discusses the pros and cons of ementoring in more detail.

With school mentoring there is probably more need for flexibility, as the schools themselves will each have different groups of pupils who have been identified as needing support in a specific area. Examples of this flexibility have been demonstrated in the provision of bilingual mentors at one school. Having a large pool of trained mentors within an HE institution can be advantageous in meeting these needs. Requests had come from schools who wished to support pupils whose native languages were Polish, Mandarin, and Twi. The pupils did not yet have a good grasp of English. Although bright, they were having difficulties in settling in and understanding the lessons. Since detailed information about all the mentors from their application forms had been retained, it was a simple matter to discover that there were undergraduate international students who had trained as mentors or coaches and who spoke these languages. With a half-day conversion training, these mentors were able to successfully work with these pupils and help them integrate into the British education system.

Another successful method for attracting mentors with a particular background was utilised for schools who wanted to encourage their pupils to stay in post-16 education. All pupils in their final year who were imminently leaving the local schools and had applied for a university place were contacted via a letter (sent to the schools). The letter invited them to apply to be a mentor should they decide to accept the university place, and it was intended that they would go back to their old school to mentor some of the younger children there, acting as a role model. This resulted in a number of these students applying to be mentors, and they found returning to their old school very rewarding. This also had the advantage that they were familiar with the school and staff where they were mentoring, which was helpful when they needed additional resources or an alternative room for mentoring to take place.

School mentoring programmes will inevitably require far more intensive supervision than when working with adults, However the impact can be transformational for many pupils. If funding can be found, then it is something that will benefit both the pupils and the mentors.

Appendix 1

Name of Scheme	
Who is to be supported?	
Why do they need support?	
Who is going to support them?	
What are the aims/objectives for the mentoring/coaching?	
How are you going to select/ identify suitable mentors or coaches?	
When will it commence?	
For how long will it last?	
What will the training plan include and who will be delivering it?	
What induction will the mentees/ coachees be given and how?	
What criteria will be used for the matching process?	
How frequently are the participants expected to meet?	
Where is it going to happen?	
How will the mentors/ coaches be supported and by whom?	
Who is going to coordinate the pro-gramme and do they have sufficient time?	
How is it going to be funded?	
How are you going to evaluate the efficacy of the mentoring/coaching?	

Appendix 2

▶ **Example Mentor/Coach Application Form**

First Name		Surname	
Preferred Name		Male/Female	
Student ID		Date of Birth	
Address (Including post/zip code)		Email address	
		Tel/Mobile	

Where did you hear about the opportunity? (poster, talk, etc.)		Year of study	
Programme of study		Grade Expected	
Undergraduate/ Postgraduate		Please state whether you are a home or international student	
State which days/ times you are free to take part in mentoring/coaching activities			

Senior School Attended		Please state if you have a part-time job and what your role is	
Education/Grades		Please state how many hours per week you work in that job	
Courses attended		Do you have use of a car during term time?	
Other interests and leisure activities		Please state any other languages you speak fluently	

Please give a statement detailing your suitability for the role, including past experiences, strengths, and what you hope to achieve by taking part.

Referee (university staff for 2nd years and above)

Name		Please ask your referee to write a reference for you that supports your application and your suitability for the role. The reference should be emailed directly to mentoringoffice@ university
Title		
Organisation		
Phone		
Email		

Appendix 3

▶ **MENTOR/COACH TRAINING**

Based on a group of 20 participants with 2 tutors or up to 12 participants and 1 tutor

AIM   To introduce the participants to the skills of mentoring or coaching, communication skills and confidentiality & disclosure. To prepare participants for issues that they might face during their sessions and to have explored the various stages of mentoring or coaching.

OBJECTIVES   By the end of the session participants will:

▶ have familiarized themselves with the aims of the mentoring or coaching programme and the skills required
▶ have set ground rules for the training days and for working with learners
▶ have discussed different types of supportive relationships and thought about the nature of a mentoring or coaching relationship
▶ have participated in exercises exploring different types of communication
▶ have learned about specific listening and questioning skills
▶ be aware of the importance of body language
▶ have explored value judgements
▶ be aware of the importance of confidentiality and disclosure
▶ be aware of how mentoring and coaching progresses through various stages and how to recognize them
▶ be comfortable with setting targets, and giving and receiving feedback
▶ have studied and discussed relevant case studies

CONTENT	METHODS	TASK	MATERIALS
1. Introductory session: ▲ Register ▲ Introduction ▲ Agenda ▲ Selection process ▲ Programme specific training	Roll call Names & roles Printed agenda & rooms	(15 min) ▲ Call register ▲ Introduce members of team ▲ Distribute agenda ▲ Introduce Aims & Objectives for the mentoring or coaching programme ▲ Explain that final selection for participation on programme will be based on observation of participants over two days of training + assessment	Attendance register Agenda Laptop Projector Screen
2. Icebreaker Group session	Participants get to know each other – discussion	(15 min) Break into pairs with someone you don't know. Find out the following information, but do not write it down (suggested questions): ▲ Who are you? / Where are you from? ▲ What are you studying? / Where do you work? ▲ What attracted you to be a mentor/coach? ▲ One person you would like to meet and why ▲ What is your best quality? ▲ One thing you disagree on ▲ What is the best thing you ever learned? Partner introduces and feeds back info to whole group	Laptop Projector Screen
3. Concerns	Individual work	(10 min) Participants write each concern they have regarding mentoring or coaching programme or the training on a Post-it. Stick them on wall. To re-visit on day 2	Post-its
4. Ground rules/ setting the boundaries Group session	Brainstorm	(10 min) Ask group for suggestions to set the ground rules for the training. Ask what needs to happen in order for the training to be successful e.g. for them to learn the skills and for you to impart all the information they need and for it to be enjoyable for everyone. Scribe onto PowerPoint. Distribute Ground Rules hand-out Discuss whether these ground rules are also appropriate within a mentoring/coaching relationship. Ensure that the issue of confidentiality/disclosure is included.	Laptop Screen Ground Rules hand-out

(Continued)

CONTENT	METHODS	TASK	MATERIALS
5. What are mentoring/ coaching? Group session	Group work Card exercise	(30 min) Divide group into 3–4. Each group is given skills cards to divide into 4: least important – most important attributes/knowledge for a mentor or coach to have. **Skills Cards examples:** Listening, Pro-active, Sense of humour, Able to give feedback, Consistency, Empathy, Sympathy, Patience, Enthusiasm, Advising, Time Management, Challenging, Action Planning, Questioning, Problem Solving, Counselling, Exploring options, Knowledge of university/organisation, Honesty, Subject Expert. After 15 mins move around to other tables to see the differences between the answers. Point out all are relevant (apart from counselling and advice giving) but are used at different times within the different stages of mentoring or coaching. Group discussion. Define 'mentoring'. Give existing examples of definitions.	Skills cards Example definitions of Mentoring or Coaching P/Point slide definitions
6. Building a relationship Group session	Small-group work	(20 mins) Divide into four groups. Each group discuss what constitutes a good relationship between any of the following and record ideas on flip-chart paper ▲ Parent – child ▲ Tutor – Student ▲ Friendship ▲ Line manager – employee ▲ Romantic relationship Stick pages on wall and one member of each team guides the whole group through their thought processes. Compare similarities and differences.	Flip-chart paper Markers Blutack
7. Assumptions	Exercise Trainer-group interaction	(10 mins) Participants are invited to say what their initial perception of the trainer was, having been given no background information (what their hobbies might be, pet owner etc.). Participants then invited to ask some questions to discover if their perceptions were correct. Discussion on how we all make pre-judgements which are in some cases totally inaccurate and best avoided when coaching and mentoring.	

8. Communication - speech Group session	Exercise Work in pairs	(20 min) Sit in pairs, back to back. A is given a picture card and describes it for B to draw. Only geometric descriptions allowed to describe the picture. B is not allowed to speak or ask questions. Simple line drawings of cat/duck, tree, house, etc. to be distributed. Use the experience to demonstrate the difficulties in communication when deprived of the ability to ask questions, clarify and see body language.	Picture cards Paper Pens/pencils
9. Listening skills Group session	Exercise in pairs	(20 min) Split group in 2. Group A leaves room and thinks of a favourite holiday to discuss. Group B instructed firstly to listen intently to partner, and on cue (finger click/cough) to stop listening or showing interest. Group A returns and group divides into A&B partners. A tells B story. General discussion. Skills noted for good listening: listening, eye contact, questioning, nodding, clarifying.	
10. Listening skills	Questionnaire	(10 min) Participants complete a listening skills questionnaire and reflect upon their areas for development	Listening skills questionnaire
11. Communication - body language	Group task and 2 x Volunteers	(15 min) Body Language – slides/photos of people interacting to discuss what they can observe Seating for mentoring/coaching – volunteers arrange seating as if for a mentoring or coaching sessions – group discussion – discuss gender differences in arrangement and appropriateness of using a table etc.	Laptop Projector Screen Body language slides and handouts
12. Listener/ speaker/ observer	Exercise in 3s	(20 min) Groups of 3: listener/speaker/observer (15mins) ▲ Speaker: talk about someone who was an influence on you ▲ Listener listens, asks questions etc ▲ Observer takes notes on what works, what doesn't, pauses, reactions, going off on a tangent etc. and gives feedback. Change position so that everyone experiences each. Feedback (5 mins each)	Paper & pens Flipchart & pen

(Continued)

CONTENT	METHODS	TASK	MATERIALS
13. Questioning Group session	Group Individually Pairs	(20 min each activity) 1. Identify types of Q's (reflective, hypothetical, probing, clarifying, multiple, rhetorical, open/closed etc.) – ask group to identify them and state if they are useful in mentoring/coaching. 2. Questioning skills sheet – poor questions for participants to rephrase 3. Work in pairs (find out interesting facts about your partner who is deliberately uncommunicative). Swap roles	Powerpoint of different example questions Questioning handout
14. Value judgements Group session	Trainer-led exercise	(15 min) Values Aim: to enforce concept that everyone has different values, that life experiences affect your decisions and opinions; do not make judgements. Set up three stations: yes/no/don't know Read out questions and participants go to station they agree with. ▲ Would you drink & drive? ▲ Would you ride a motorbike? ▲ Would you read someone's diary? ▲ Would you have an affair? ▲ Would you tell a friend if their partner was having an affair? ▲ Would you report your friend if they had cheated in an exam? ▲ Would you keep a £20.00 note if you found it on a supermarket floor? Participants explain the reasons for their choices whilst others listen and respect their opinions.	
15. Disclosure Group session	Case studies	(20 min) Divide into groups. Give 3 different case studies to discuss. Groups feedback on whether they would 'disclose' in each scenario	Laptop Projector Screen Case studies (Child Protection Guidelines if appropriate)

16. Common issues Group session	Group Individually	(20 min) Acetates with common issues and flipchart paper on walls. Participants go around individually and write down on the flipchart paper possible courses of action/questions to ask to deal with the common issues. Examples – My coachee keeps arriving late to our sessions; My mentee is very talkative taking the focus away from the subject in hand; Although my mentee comes to the sessions they are uncommunicative; I don't think my coachee is being entirely honest about their exam results. Group feedback.	
17. Goal Setting Feedback Group Session	PowerPoint	(15 min) Explanation of Kolb's theory of experiential learning and how this relates to a mentoring or coaching relationship. The mentor/coach facilitates this learning process. Explain SMART targets. Give participants good & bad examples of completed logbooks on PowerPoint.	Kolb handout SMART targets presentation Sample logbook on PowerPoint. Laptop Screen Projector
18. Feedback Group Session	Exercise in pairs	(20 min) In pairs A tells B about something that really irritates them and why (people littering in the street, smoking in cars, etc.) whilst B listens. B then feeds back all the positive information that they have gleaned to A. PowerPoint on giving and receiving feedback – how to maintain self-esteem and the importance of obtaining and dealing with regular feedback from your learner.	Powerpoint
19. Preparing for the 1st session Group session	Trainer-led discussion	(10 min) Group should be asked to reflect on what they would like to know about THEIR mentor or coach prior to meeting them IF they were to apply. What preparation is required for the 1st session? Ensure that the point is made that they should not have too much information on their learner prior to meeting but to allow them to tell their 'story' and ambitions in their own words.	Laptop Projector Screen

(Continued)

CONTENT	METHODS	TASK	MATERIALS
20. Mentor/Coach promotion Group Session	PowerPoint Group Individual	(15 min) Show examples of poor mentor or coach profiles. Ask why they are poor. Show good examples and stress importance of honesty and learner perspective when selecting the coach/mentor of their choice. Distribute profile form for participants to complete	Blank profile forms
21. Mentoring tools Group Session	PowerPoint	(10 min) Demonstrate some common mentoring or coaching tools and some contexts in which they could be used.	Mentoring/coaching toolkits
22. Applying tools to common issues Group session	Group discussion and feedback	(20 min) Using acetates and flipchart paper from previous session, participants revisit the common issues and in small group suggest a SMART target that could be set and two possible mentoring/coaching tools that could be used.	Acetates Flipchart paper. Different coloured pens.
23. Real play Group session	Work in 3s	(40 min) Real play mini-mentoring or coaching session using a real issue to include a SMART target or use of a coaching/mentoring tool if possible. Rotate so that each person has the opportunity to be a coach/mentor, a learner and an observer. The observer gives appropriate feedback to the coach/mentor following each practise session.	Observation and reflection sheets
24. Assessment	Individual	(30 min) Each participant given a short scenario and asked to write down how they would deal with it. The answers should incorporate examples of questions that they would ask, possible SMART targets and suggested mentoring/coaching tools that could be used.	Evaluation form Training dates hand-out
25. Plenary	Whole group	(15 min) Review of post-it notes from Day 1 – are the concerns still valid? Further training requirements Collect feedback/evaluation Explain next steps (when they can expect to be matched)	Evaluation form Training dates hand-out

Appendix 4

▶ **LISTENING SKILLS – SELF EVALUATION**

Are you a good Listener?

Think carefully about how you listen to people.
Circle the response that you feel is the most accurate answer.
Be as honest as possible.

ATTITUDES	Almost Always	Usually	Some-times	Seldom	Almost Never
Do you like to listen to other people talk?	5	4	3	2	1
Do you listen regardless of a speaker's manner of speech and choice of words?	5	4	3	2	1
Do you listen even if you do not like the person who is speaking?	5	4	3	2	1
Are you able to listen equally well regardless of the speaker's race, gender, or age?	5	4	3	2	1
Do you listen equally well to friend, stranger, or acquaintance?	5	4	3	2	1
CAPABILITY – SKILLS					
Do you put what you have been doing out of sight and mind?	5	4	3	2	1
Do you look at the speaker?	5	4	3	2	1
Are you able to ignore the distractions around you?	5	4	3	2	1
Do you smile, nod your head, and otherwise encourage the speaker to talk?	5	4	3	2	1
Do you think about what the speaker is saying?	5	4	3	2	1
Do you try to figure out what the speaker means?	5	4	3	2	1
If the speaker hesitates, do you encourage them to go on?	5	4	3	2	1

(Continued)

ATTITUDES	Almost Always	Usually	Some-times	Seldom	Almost Never
Do you restate what the speaker says, then ask if you got the meaning right?	5	4	3	2	1
Do you withhold judgement about a speaker's idea until they have finished?	5	4	3	2	1
Do you encourage a hesitant speaker to talk?	5	4	3	2	1
Do you listen even if you anticipate what the speaker is going to say?	5	4	3	2	1
Do you question the speaker in order to encourage them to explain their idea more fully?	5	4	3	2	1
Do you ask the speaker what the words mean as they use them?	5	4	3	2	1

Add up your total points and enter the figure here

- ▶ Answers where you scored less than 3 will show you in which ways you can improve your listening skills
- ▶ If you rated yourself with a score of less than 50, you will need to consciously make an effort to improve your listening skills

Appendix 5

▶ **Example of a Mentee Profile Form**

Please note that the information you provide on this form is for matching purposes only. Your personal details will not be given to your mentor or coach without your consent.

First Name		**Family name**	
Name you prefer to be called		**Male/Female**	
Student number		**Date of Birth**	__ / __ / __
Address		**Email**	
		Tel/Mobile	
Ethnic Background *(optional)*			
Disability *(optional)*	YES/NO		
Course/Year of Study			
Hobbies/Interests			
List any mentor preferences *(e.g. male/female, course, age etc.)*			
Name of 1st choice mentor:		**Name of 2nd choice mentor:**	

With which of these academic tasks could a mentor help you? Tick all that apply.

Time management	☐	Referencing my work	☐
Structuring assignments	☐	Presenting assignments	
Conducting research		Revision	
Writing essays		Exam preparation	
Group work		Other (please specify): _____	

With which of these aspects of student life could a mentor help you? Tick all that apply.

Living in halls or off-campus ☐
Budgeting
Getting the study/social balance right
Information about clubs, societies, and university facilities
Paid employment or work placements
Other (please specify): _____

Is there anything you would like your mentor to be aware of? (e.g. dyslexia, mobility, hearing impairment, etc.)

References

ACKLAND, R. 1991. A Review of the Peer Coaching Literature. *Journal of Staff Development*, 12, 22–27.

ANDREWS, J., & CLARK, R. 2011. Peer Mentoring Works: How Peer Mentoring Enhances Success in Higher Education. Aston University.

BOUD, D., COHEN, R. & SAMPSON, J. (2001) *Peer Learning in Higher Education: Learning from and with Each Other*, London: Routledge Falmer.

CAPSTICK, S., FLEMING, H., & HURNE, J. 2004. Implementing Peer-Assisted Learning in Higher Education: The Experience of a New University and a Model for the Achievement of a Mainstream Programme in Peer-Assisted Learning. Conference Proceedings, Bournemouth University.

CHAO, G. T. 1998. Invited Reaction: Challenging Research in Mentoring. *Human Resource Development Quarterly*, 9, 333–338.

Chao, G. T. Professional Psychology: Research and Practice, Vol 40(3), Jun 2009, 314–320.

CLUTTERBUCK, D., & MEGGINSON, D. 1999. *Mentoring Executives and Directors*, Oxford: Butterworth Heinemann.

COLVIN, J., & ASHMAN, M. 2010. Roles, Risks and Benefits of Peer Mentoring Relationships in Higher Education. *Mentoring and Tutoring: Partnership in Learning*, 18, 121–134.

CROZIER, R. 1997. *Individual Learners: Personality Differences in Education*, London: Routledge.

DONEGAN, M., OSTROSKY, M., & FOWLER, S. 2000. Peer Coaching: Teachers Supporting Teachers. *Young Exceptional Children*, 3, Spring, 9–16.

FOSKETT, N., ROBERTS, D., & MARINGE, F. 2006. Changing Fee Regimes and Their Impact on Student Attitudes to Higher Education. *Report of a Higher Education Academy-Funded Research Project 2005–2006*. University of Southampton.

GREEN, P. 2011. A Literature Review of Peer-Assisted Learning (PAL). *National HE STEM Programme Project – Peer Assisted Learning: In and beyond the Classroom*. University of Bath.

HALL, A. 2008. *The S-Factor: A Coaching Handbook*, Oxford: Oxford Professional Consulting Ltd.

HILL, R., & REDDY, P. 2007. Undergraduate Peer Mentoring: An Investigation into Processes, Activities and Outcomes. *Psychology Learning and Teaching*, 6, 98–103.

HONEY, P., & MUMFORD, A. 2006. *The Learning Styles Helper's Guide*, Maidenhead, Berkshire: Peter Honey Publications.

HUSBAND, P., & JACOBS, P. 2009. Peer Mentoring in Higher Education: A Review of the Current Literature and Recommendations for Implementation of Mentoring Schemes. *The Plymouth Student Scientist*, 2, 228–241.

IVES, Y. 2008. What Is 'Coaching'? An Exploration of Conflicting Paradigms. *International Journal of Evidence-Based Coaching and Mentoring*, 6, 100.

JACOBI, M. 1991. Mentoring and Undergraduate Academic Success: A Literature Review. *Review of Educational Research*, Winter, 505–532.

KOLB, D. A. 1984. *Experiential Learning: Experience as the Source of Learning and Development*, Englewood Cliffs, NJ: Prentice-Hall.

LEIDENFROST, B., STRASSNIG, B., SCHABMANN, A., SPIEL, C., & CARBON, C. 2011. Peer-Mentoring Styles and Their Contribution to Academic Success among Mentees:

A Person-Oriented Study in Higher Education. *Mentoring and Tutoring: Partnership in Learning*, 19, 347–364.

PARSLOE, E., & WRAY, M. 2000. *Coaching and Mentoring*, London: Kogan Page.

PICKLES, T. 1992. *Dealing with Disaffection: Practical Responses to School-Related Issues*, London: Longman.

PITKETHLY, M., & PROSSER, M. 2001. The First-Year Experience Project: A Model for University-Wide Change. *Higher education Research and Development*, 20, 185.

QUINN, F., MULDOON, R., & HOLLINGWORTH, A. 2002. Formal Academic Mentoring: A Pilot Scheme for First-Year Science Students at a Regional University. *Mentoring & Tutoring for Partnership in Learning*, 10, 21–33.

RICHARDSON, J. T. E. 1990. Reliability and Replicability of the Approaches to Studying Questionnaire. *Studies in Higher Education*, 15, 155–168.

ROGERS, J. 2004. *Coaching Skills: A Handbook*, London: Open University Press.

ROSENBERG, M. 1965. *Society and the Adolescent Self-Image*, Princeton University Press.

SALTER, K., & TWIDLE, R. 2010. *The Learning Mentor's Resources Book*, London: Sage Publications.

SANDER, P., & SANDERS, L. 2006. Understanding Academic Confidence. *Psychology Teaching Review*, 12.

SCHEIN, E. 1990. *Career Anchors (discovering your real values)*, San Francisco: Jossey-Bass Pfeiffer.

STOBER, D., & GRANT, A. M. 2006. *Toward a Contextual Approach to Coaching Models*, New York: Wiley.

THOMAS, L. 2012. A Summary of Findings and Recommendations from the What Works? Student Retention and Success Programme, Paul Hamlyn Foundation, London.

TOPPING, K. 1996. The Effectiveness of Peer Tutoring in Further and Higher Education: A Typology and Review of the Literature. *Higher Education*, 32, 321–345.

WHITMORE, J. 2002. *Coaching for Performance*, London: Nicholas Brealey Publishing.

Index